DISEASES & DISORDERS

Fibromyalgia

Melissa Abramovitz

LUCENT BOOKS

A part of Gale, Cengage Learning

GALE
CENGAGE Learning

Detroit • New York • San Francisco • New Haven, Conn • Waterville, Maine • London

LIBRARY OF CONGRESS CATALOGING-IN-PUBLICATION DATA

Abramovitz, Melissa, 1954-
  Fibromyalgia / Melissa Abramovitz.
    p. cm. -- (Diseases and disorders)
  Summary: "This series objectively and thoughtfully explores topics of medical importance. Books include sections on a description of the disease or disorder and how it affects the body, as well as diagnosis and treatment of the condition"-- Provided by publisher.
  Includes bibliographical references and index.
  ISBN 978-1-4205-0673-0 (hardback)
  1. Fibromyalgia--Juvenile literature. I. Title.
  RC927.3.A27 2011
  616.7'42--dc23
                                                            2011020763

Lucent Books
27500 Drake Rd.
Farmington Hills, MI 48331

ISBN-13: 978-1-4205-0673-0
ISBN-10: 1-4205-0673-0

Table of Contents

"The Most Difficult Puzzles Ever Devised"

Charles Best, one of the pioneers in the search for a cure for diabetes, once explained what it is about medical research that intrigued him so. "It's not just the gratification of knowing one is helping people," he confided, "although that probably is a more heroic and selfless motivation. Those feelings may enter in, but truly, what I find best is the feeling of going toe to toe with nature, of trying to solve the most difficult puzzles ever devised. The answers are there somewhere, those keys that will solve the puzzle and make the patient well. But how will those keys be found?"

Since the dawn of civilization, nothing has so puzzled people—and often frightened them, as well—as the onset of illness in a body or mind that had seemed healthy before. A seizure, the inability of a heart to pump, the sudden deterioration of muscle tone in a small child—being unable to reverse such conditions or even to understand why they occur was unspeakably frustrating to healers. Even before there were names for such conditions, even before they were understood at all, each was a reminder of how complex the human body was, and how vulnerable.

While our grappling with understanding diseases has been frustrating at times, it has also provided some of humankind's most heroic accomplishments. Alexander Fleming's accidental discovery in 1928 of a mold that could be turned into penicillin has resulted in the saving of untold millions of lives. The isolation of the enzyme insulin has reversed what was once a death sentence for anyone with diabetes. There have been great strides in combating conditions for which there is not yet a cure, too. Medicines can help AIDS patients live longer, diagnostic tools such as mammography and ultrasounds can help doctors find tumors while they are treatable, and laser surgery techniques have made the most intricate, minute operations routine.

This "toe-to-toe" competition with diseases and disorders is even more remarkable when seen in a historical continuum. An astonishing amount of progress has been made in a very short time. Just two hundred years ago, the existence of germs as a cause of some diseases was unknown. In fact, it was less than 150 years ago that a British surgeon named Joseph Lister had difficulty persuading his fellow doctors that washing their hands before delivering a baby might increase the chances of a healthy delivery (especially if they had just attended to a diseased patient)!

Each book in Lucent's Diseases and Disorders series explores a disease or disorder and the knowledge that has been accumulated (or discarded) by doctors through the years. Each book also examines the tools used for pinpointing a diagnosis, as well as the various means that are used to treat or cure a disease. Finally, new ideas are presented—techniques or medicines that may be on the horizon.

Frustration and disappointment are still part of medicine, for not every disease or condition can be cured or prevented. But the limitations of knowledge are being pushed outward constantly; the "most difficult puzzles ever devised" are finding challengers every day.

A Controversial Disease

The American Medical Association recognized fibromyalgia (FM), which involves widespread pain, fatigue, and overly sensitive nerves, as a disease in 1987. The World Health Organization established fibromyalgia as an official disease in 1993. However, many medical experts still contend that fibromyalgia is not a real disease.

One reason for this controversy is that diagnosing fibromyalgia is primarily subjective. "As of now, there are no laboratory tests, no imaging methods, no electrical tests—no tests of any kind—that define fibromyalgia,"[1] explains fibromyalgia expert M. Clement Hall in *The Fibromyalgia Controversy*. Instead, diagnosis depends on a patient's reported symptoms and on a physician's expertise.

Unlike many diseases that have obvious physical signs such as inflammation, sores, lumps, tissue damage, or abnormal body chemistry, fibromyalgia does not have similar outward or inward signs. A doctor relies on a patient's reports of unseen qualities such as pain when he or she applies pressure to certain areas of the patient's body.

Rheumatologist George E. Ehrlich of the University of Pennsylvania and many other experts believe that fibromyalgia is nothing more than a contrived diagnosis for vague, unproved symptoms such as reported pain. In an article appearing in the

Journal of Rheumatology, Ehrlich writes that while patients' pain is real, fibromyalgia is not: "When one has tuberculosis, one has tuberculosis, whether or not it is diagnosed. The same is true for cancer, rheumatoid arthritis, hookworm infestation—really, of the gamut of diseases. But not for fibromyalgia (FM). No one has fibromyalgia until it is diagnosed."[2]

A Wastebasket Diagnosis

Doctors who believe that fibromyalgia is not a real disease argue that it has become a "wastebasket" diagnosis applied to patients, particularly in certain cultures, with symptoms that cannot be explained by other diseases. As Ehrlich writes: "Everybody has pain sometimes, and even chronic pain during a lifetime. In Western cities, FM tends to be diagnosed when no other reason is found for the pain. The same pains in rural areas or developing countries go unmarked, and people get on with their lives."[3]

Angela Mailis, director of a pain clinic at the University of Toronto Hospital in Canada, agrees with this contention and also states in *The Fibromyalgia Controversy* that fibromyalgia does not possess qualities that make it a separate, well-defined disease. "As a lifelong student of chronic pain, I have had a hard time accepting fibromyalgia as a specific, definable entity, and I am not alone," she explains. "All the symptoms attributed to fibromyalgia do not necessarily constitute a condition that is scientifically specific."[4]

Along these same lines, some experts believe that fibromyalgia has become a catch-all diagnosis for people who imagine that they are sick but who have nothing physically wrong. Such experts refer to fibromyalgia patients as hypochondriacs or as having somatization disorder, which is a general term for chronic physical symptoms for which no physical cause can be found. Rheumatologist Nortin M. Hadler of the University of North Carolina at Chapel Hill writes in a *Journal of Rheumatology* article that diagnosing a patient with fibromyalgia reinforces and perpetuates the individual's imagined symptoms: "FM is a form of illness behavior . . . it is the medicalization

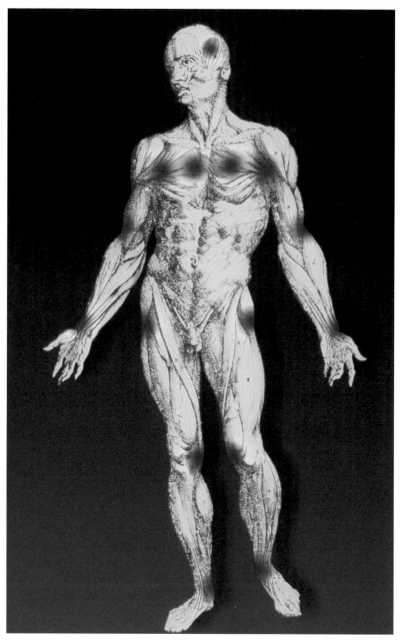

Fibromyalgia is a musculoskeletal pain and fatigue disorder
for which there is no known cause. The illustration highlights
fibromyalgia-induced pain point areas. The diagnosis and
treatment of fibromyalgia is controversial.

of misery . . . people choose to be patients because they have exhausted their wherewithal to cope."[5]

Fibromyalgia and Disability Lawsuits

Hand in hand with its reputation as a contrived, wastebasket disease, fibromyalgia has become embroiled in a medical-legal controversy that some experts say further diminishes its standing as a real disease. Some patients try to use a diagnosis of fibromyalgia as a method of being declared disabled so they can collect disability benefits, and others claim that a minor traffic accident caused their fibromyalgia. Such individuals then argue that they are entitled to monetary compensation from insurance companies or people who caused the accident.

Evidence abounds that some lawyers and disability advocates have coached patients to say "ouch" when a doctor presses on certain so-called tender points so the doctor will diagnose fibromyalgia. There is also evidence that some doctors are fooled by patients' complaints and diagnose fibromyalgia when nothing is really wrong. Furthermore, several studies have found that minor car accidents that occur in places where disability benefits or other compensation is available are far more likely to result in claims of permanent pain and disability than are accidents in other places. In his book *Whiplash and Other Useful Illnesses*, Canadian psychiatrist Andrew Malleson concluded that fibromyalgia was one "useful" illness that lawyers, doctors, and patients have exploited to receive monetary awards in places where compensation is popular. Other experts who doubt the legitimacy of fibromyalgia agree with this assessment. "We have turned a common symptom [pain] into a remunerative industry,"[6] Ehrlich writes.

The Other Viewpoint

While acknowledging that a diagnosis of fibromyalgia has been occasionally abused for financial gain, experts who argue that fibromyalgia is indeed a real disease point out that most patients simply want an answer about why they are experiencing the often debilitating symptoms that go along with the disorder. These authorities also state that fibromyalgia differs from other conditions that involve pain, and they find that patients are not imagining that something is wrong. "The severity of the condition known as fibromyalgia has justified it being named,"[7] writes Hall.

Furthermore, recent scientific studies indicate that many people with fibromyalgia have abnormal levels of certain brain chemicals such as serotonin and norepinephrine, as well as abnormal function in some areas of the brain and spinal cord. "Contemporary research is hot on the track of unraveling the changes that occur in the nervous system of fibromyalgia patients. The basic message is that fibromyalgia cannot be considered a primarily psychological disorder,"[8] writes fibro-myalgia expert Robert M. Bennett in a National Fibromyalgia Association article. Some of these changes may not be specific to fibromyalgia, but some appear to be unique. If researchers can develop objective laboratory tests to determine who has these disease-specific abnormalities, this will no doubt en-hance the legitimacy of fibromyalgia. But until this happens, the controversy over whether fibromyalgia is a real disease is most likely to continue.

CHAPTER ONE

What Is Fibromyalgia?

Descriptions of diseases that resemble what is now known as fibromyalgia have been found in the medical and popular literature for thousands of years. Some fibromyalgia experts believe that Job's description of his medical problems in the Bible indicate that he may have had fibromyalgia, though there is no proof of this. Job says in the book of Job: "I, too, have been assigned months of futility, long and weary nights of misery. When I go to bed, I think, 'When will it be morning?' But the night drags on, and I toss till dawn. . . . And now my heart is broken. Depression haunts my days. My weary nights are filled with pain as though something were relentlessly gnawing at my bones."[9]

Some modern doctors claim that Hans Christian Andersen's classic story "The Princess and the Pea" describes a woman with fibromyalgia who was so sensitive to pain that a pea placed underneath a pile of mattresses hurt her. However, no one knows whether or not Andersen was referring to a particular disease or was just using his imagination when he wrote this story.

The writings of medical doctors over the centuries provide more substantial evidence that fibromyalgia has existed throughout human history. Doctors beginning with the Greek physician Galen have described a fibromyalgia-like disease that involved widespread pain and fatigue. Around A.D. 199 Galen wrote that this unnamed disorder resulted from a humor, or chemical, called rheuma that flowed through the body.

Some doctors have used as a metaphor for fibromyalgia the fairy tale of "The Princess and the Pea," about a young princess who complained of discomfort from a pea that lay at the bottom of her bed of many mattresses.

In 1816 the Scottish surgeon William Balfour first revealed that a disease widely known since the 1600s as muscular rheumatism included painful tender points throughout the body, and in 1869 neurologist George Beard wrote about a disease he called neurasthenia. Symptoms of neurasthenia included fainting, sleep problems, headaches, sensitive muscles and skin, gastrointestinal problems, and back pain. Many modern experts believe that both muscular rheumatism and neurasthenia were most likely what is now known as fibromyalgia.

In 1904 the British neurologist William Gowers wrote the first formal description of a disease he named fibrositis, and doctors later changed the name to fibromyalgia. Thus, fibrositis is the first disease that experts are sure is the same as the one now known as fibromyalgia. Gowers called the disorder fibrositis because he believed that inflammation (*itis*) of the muscle fibers (*fibro*) was producing overly sensitive nerves and pain in affected people.

It was not until 1981 that rheumatologist Muhammad Yunus of the University of Illinois School of Medicine proved that people with fibrositis did not have inflammation in their muscles. Yunus then changed the name of the disease to fibromyalgia. The Latin root *fibra* means "fibrous tissue," *myos* means "muscle," and *algos* means "pain." The name of the disease reveals that the main symptom patients experience is pain in their muscles.

Fibromyalgia Today

Doctors today refer to the disease as either fibromyalgia or fibromyalgia syndrome (FMS). A syndrome is a collection of symptoms that people with a particular medical condition share. Technically, fibromyalgia is a syndrome rather than a disease, but most experts do not make this distinction.

About 10 million people in the United States and 3 to 6 percent of the world's population have fibromyalgia. Most are women of childbearing age, but many men, children, and older women also have the disease. Women are diagnosed with fibromyalgia approximately twenty times more frequently than men are.

Fibromyalgia occurs in all ethnic and racial groups and affects people in all states of health and fitness. However, people who are overweight and who do not exercise regularly are about twice as likely to develop fibromyalgia as others are.

William Gowers

William Gowers was born in London in 1845. At age fifteen he began serving as a physician's apprentice and became interested in studying chemistry and biology. He graduated from the University of London at age eighteen and enrolled in medical school. Although Gowers came from a poor family and did not have the money to pay for medical school, friends who wanted to help him succeed because of his intelligence and work ethic introduced him to William Jenner at the Royal College of Physicians. Jenner was impressed with Gowers and hired him as his secretary, so Gowers was able to support himself while he attended medical school.

After earning his medical degree, Gowers became a physician and teacher at the University College Hospital. There he published numerous articles and invented new methods of counting blood cells in blood tests. In 1888 he joined the staff at the National Hospital and devoted the remainder of his career to studying the nervous system. His textbook, *Manual of Diseases of the Nervous System*, contained one of the first detailed descriptions of all the known nervous system disorders and gained

But being physically fit certainly does not prevent fibromyalgia. One fibromyalgia patient named Bill, for example, was a competitive cyclist when he developed fibromyalgia in his twenties.

Not only can fibromyalgia strike anyone at any time during their lives, its course and progression are also unpredictable and vary from person to person. Different patients have mild, moderate, or severe symptoms, and the severity can vary over time and change without warning. But whatever its severity, fibromyalgia is almost always chronic, or long lasting. Symptoms may wax and wane, but the condition does not go away. However, fibromyalgia does not damage tissues and is not fatal.

notoriety because of the manner in which he incorporated his experiences with patients into the text. Medical experts called it the "Bible of neurology." In 1897 Queen Victoria knighted Gowers for his medical contributions.

In 1904 Gowers published an article in the *British Medical Journal* about a condition characterized by widespread pain, exhaustion, and an inability to sleep. He called it fibrositis because he believed it resulted from inflammation in the muscles. Experts later proved it did not involve inflammation and changed the name of the disease to fibromyalgia.

British scientist Willam Gower invented the haemoglobinometer kit for testing blood in 1875. He would go on to write the first detailed descriptions of the then-known nervous system disorders.

Universal Symptoms

Although the intensity and nature of symptoms may vary among patients, fibromyalgia always includes pain, fatigue, and oversensitivity to certain sensations. Explains fibromyalgia expert William S. Wilke in *The Cleveland Clinic Guide to Fibromyalgia*:

> There is always widespread pain that has existed over a period of months. There are no exceptions: fibromyalgia hurts every day.

> And there is always fatigue, almost always accompanied by sleep disturbances. We're not talking about feeling

tired after a couple long days at work. We're talking about a continuing energy level so low that . . . you feel your batteries have run down.[10]

Most people with fibromyalgia have widespread pain on waking in the morning, as well as at other times. Activity and cold weather seem to worsen the pain. Many patients describe the pain as burning, throbbing, or stabbing in muscles and joints. Pain can occur anywhere in the body, but the most common sites are the neck, back, shoulders, hands, and pelvic area.

The third hallmark symptom of fibromyalgia is known as central nervous system sensitization. The central nervous system consists of the brain and spinal cord. According to the Mayo Clinic, "Researchers believe that fibromyalgia amplifies painful sensations by affecting the way your brain processes pain signals."[11] Nerves in the brain and spinal cord become more sensitive not only to pain, but also to sensations that would not bother other people. Lights may seem too bright, sounds too loud, and smells, taste, and touch overwhelming

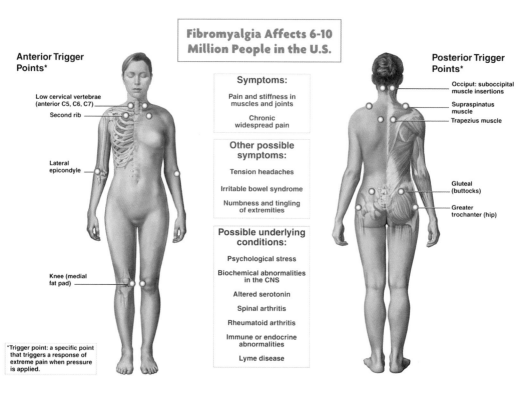

Fibromyalgia Affects 6-10 Million People in the U.S.

Anterior Trigger Points*

Low cervical vertebrae (anterior C5, C6, C7)

Second rib

Lateral epicondyle

Knee (medial fat pad)

Posterior Trigger Points*

Occiput: suboccipital muscle insertions

Supraspinatus muscle

Trapezius muscle

Gluteal (buttocks)

Greater trochanter (hip)

Symptoms:

Pain and stiffness in muscles and joints

Chronic widespread pain

Other possible symptoms:

Tension headaches

Irritable bowel syndrome

Numbness and tingling of extremities

Possible underlying conditions:

Psychological stress

Biochemical abnormalities in the CNS

Altered serotonin

Spinal arthritis

Rheumatoid arthritis

Immune or endocrine abnormalities

Lyme disease

*Trigger point: a specific point that triggers a response of extreme pain when pressure is applied.

to people with fibromyalgia. Experts refer to the condition in which sensations that are not normally unpleasant seem painful as allodynia.

One patient described her hypersensitivity like this: "My clothes began to hurt. I would lie in bed and then change from one nightgown to another. . . . It was like my blood was on fire."[12]

Tissues and organs throughout the body, in addition to sensory organs, may become hypersensitive, and severe pain may result from overstimulated nerves in these places. This can lead to cramping in the intestines, a frequent need to urinate when the bladder is affected, or shortness of breath when nerves in the heart and lungs are involved. Sensitization in the brain can lead to dizziness when the individual stands up after sitting or lying down and to cognitive (thinking) problems. The brain becomes overwhelmed by all the incoming sights, sounds, tastes, smells, or touch sensations and cannot concentrate on simple things like reading a book or cooking a meal. Experts refer to this as fibro-fog. The amount of fibro-fog seems to be directly related to the amount of pain and the intensity of an individual's sleep problems. People with severe pain and sleep problems are most likely to become confused, lost, and unable to perform everyday tasks.

Parallel and Overlapping Conditions

Many people with fibromyalgia also have one or more other medical conditions, and these overlapping conditions can exacerbate symptoms of fibromyalgia or add symptoms of their own to the mix. It is often difficult for doctors to distinguish which symptoms result from fibromyalgia and which result from the other disorders. This can make diagnosis and treatment of fibromyalgia challenging.

Many, if not most, fibromyalgia patients, for example, are also clinically depressed. Depression affects the body, thoughts, and mood. People who are depressed feel hopeless, helpless, and often anxious. They do not enjoy life and often have trouble sleeping, concentrating, and remembering things.

Overview of Fibromyalgia

Statistics

About 10 million Americans suffer from fibromyalgia. Most are women of child-bearing age, but anyone of any age can get the disease.

Causes

A genetic prediposition and environmental triggers such as stress interact to cause fibromyalgia.

Symptoms

Pain, fatigue, and oversensitive nerves.

Diagnosis

Widespread pain in all four quadrants of the body for at least three months and tenderness in at least 11 of 18 standardized tender points.

Exercise Programs

Regular moderate exercise such as walking or swimming is important in any treatment plan.

Treatment

Drugs, physical therapy, education, proper nutrition, and regular exercise are all accepted elements of treatment.

In patients who have both fibromyalgia and depression, the sleep and cognitive difficulties can result from either disorder.

Another condition that frequently coexists with fibromyalgia is headaches. About 70 percent of fibromyalgia patients have recurring tension or migraine headaches. As well as involving severe pain, migraines can also include hypersensitivity to light and sound, and distinguishing which disease is responsible for such symptoms may be important in assessing treatment options.

About 25 percent of people with fibromyalgia also have irritable bowel syndrome (IBS), which is characterized by bloating, abdominal cramps, diarrhea, and constipation. Studies have shown that people with IBS tend to process signals from the intestines in different brain areas than most people do, and this may make them more sensitive to gastrointestinal pain. It may be that people with both fibromyalgia and IBS have a generalized hypersensitivity that makes them vulnerable to both disorders.

Another disorder that often co-occurs with fibromyalgia is restless leg syndrome. Here an individual has constant urges to move the legs when they are at rest, especially at night. When people with restless leg syndrome also have fibromyalgia, this can exacerbate any sleep disturbances.

Many women with fibromyalgia also have painful menstrual periods, and some also have interstitial cystitis, which involves a loss of the mucous lining of the bladder that results in severe pain and frequent urination. Doctors are not sure whether these conditions include hypersensitivity to pain when they occur without fibromyalgia.

Eighty-five percent of people with fibromyalgia also have temporomandibular dysfunction (TMD). This involves pain in the muscles and bones of the head, neck, jaw, and face. TMD makes chewing food extremely painful. As with other diseases that co-occur with fibromyalgia, TMD raises the patient's overall pain level. But because symptoms of TMD are confined to one area of the body, it is usually not difficult for a doctor to determine whether or not a patient has TMD.

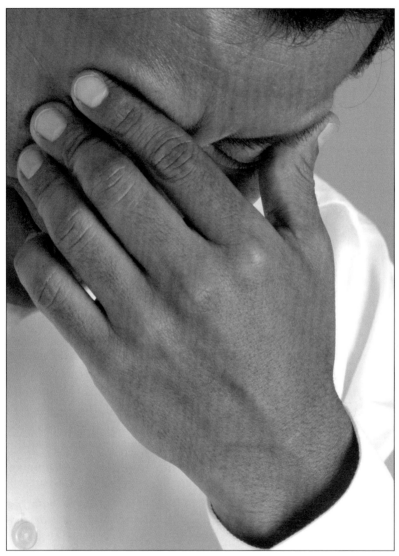

Migraine headaches frequently coexist with fibromyalgia. Migraines cause severe pain and hypersensitivity to light and sound.

Diseases Similar to Fibromyalgia

Besides being associated with these overlapping conditions, fibromyalgia can mimic a variety of other diseases that involve widespread pain and fatigue. This is another factor that makes fibromyalgia difficult to diagnose. To further complicate matters, fibromyalgia sometimes co-occurs with the diseases it may mimic.

One group of disorders that fibromyalgia can mimic is autoimmune disorders, such as rheumatoid arthritis, multiple sclerosis, and lupus. Autoimmune diseases result from the body's immune system mistakenly attacking its own cells. Like fibromyalgia, some of these diseases involve widespread pain, fatigue, sleep problems, depression, and varying degrees of disability. But autoimmune diseases are characterized by inflammation and by antibodies to the self, and fibromyalgia is not. Once doctors perform laboratory and imaging tests for inflammation and for antibodies to the self, they can usually diagnose an autoimmune disease if one is present. Sometimes, though, these tests are inconclusive. For instance, based on inconclusive tests, doctors initially diagnosed a patient named Jane with multiple sclerosis but later changed the diagnosis to fibromyalgia when further tests ruled out inflammation.

Having an autoimmune disease raises the risk of developing fibromyalgia; thus people who already have an autoimmune disease are more likely than other people to also end up with fibromyalgia. When someone does have both, this tends to worsen the symptoms of each disease. These factors further complicate the challenges of diagnosing and treating both disorders.

Another disease that often mimics fibromyalgia is chronic fatigue syndrome. This disease is primarily characterized by overwhelming fatigue that is not relieved by sleep or rest. But it can also include mood disorders, memory and concentration problems, headaches, fever, sore throat, feeling sick after exercise, and muscle and joint pain. As is the case with fibromyalgia, there are no laboratory tests that can diagnose chronic fatigue syndrome, and many doctors have difficulty distinguishing the two disorders. Some patients are eventually diagnosed with both fibromyalgia and chronic fatigue syndrome.

Post-traumatic stress disorder (PTSD) and a related disorder called Gulf War syndrome also share some qualities with fibromyalgia and may be confused with it. PTSD and Gulf War syndrome affect people who have experienced a traumatic or stressful event such as being in a war or being a crime victim. Besides having fatigue, sleep problems, diffuse pain, mood disorders, and cognitive difficulties, people with PTSD and Gulf War syndrome have terrifying flashbacks to the traumatic

Chronic fatigue syndrome often mimics fibromyalgia in symptoms that include overwhelming fatigue not relieved by sleep or rest, feeling sick after exercise, mood disorders, concentration and memory problems, fever, headaches, and muscle and joint pain.

incident that triggered the disease. The presence of these flash-backs is usually enough to allow doctors to distinguish these conditions from fibromyalgia. But recent studies indicate that PTSD itself can lead to fibromyalgia, so the distinctions may become muddied.

Other Difficulties in Diagnosis

The confusion that can result from diseases that mimic fibro-myalgia often means that patients do not receive an accurate diagnosis for some time. "Because of the lack of specific char-acterizing features, and the wide spectrum of medical problems covered by pain and fatigue, it is unusual for a patient to be diagnosed with fibromyalgia the first time she expresses her problems to a healthcare provider,"[13] states M. Clement Hall in *The Fibromyalgia Controversy*. Indeed, a 2007 study reported that half of the people eventually diagnosed with fibromyalgia consulted more than three doctors, and on average the diagno-sis took five years.

Many times diagnosis is also delayed because many doctors do not take patients' claims of vague symptoms seriously. Cic-ely, a young grandmother who began experiencing widespread pain, fatigue, and trouble sleeping after her daughter left her own children with Cicely, said that when she complained about her symptoms, her doctor laughed and told her that six children would do that to anyone.

Melissa S. Herman, who developed symptoms at age nine-teen, was not diagnosed with fibromyalgia until she was twenty-six, because doctors did not take her complaints seriously. She writes:

> I was 19 and doctors were telling me I was crazy and that nothing was wrong with me. It was "all in my head." So, not only was I suffering from an illness that was difficult to diagnose, but I was surrounded by doctors who used my youth and gender against me. Yes, my gender too. I was in the process of getting married at the time and one doctor said it was just "nerves." I thought the dark ages were behind us when "hysteria" was the cause of a woman's ills![14]

Many times a diagnosis of fibromyalgia is also delayed because the doctors a patient consults are not familiar with the disease, and sometimes the delay occurs because the physicians believe that fibromyalgia is not a real disease. Thus, fibromyalgia experts say it is important for patients who suspect fibromyalgia to consult a doctor who has extensive experience diagnosing and treating the disorder. Although some primary care doctors, such as family practitioners or internists, have this experience, most of the time specialists called rheumatologists have the most expertise. Rheumatologists specialize in diseases that involve pain or inflammation in the muscles, joints, and tendons and ligaments that attach bones to other bones and to muscles. Some neurologists, who specialize in the nervous system, have expertise in fibromyalgia as well.

The Diagnostic Process

The first step in the diagnostic process is the medical history. The physician questions the patient about his or her symptoms, other diseases, medications he or she takes, and lifestyle habits such as smoking, drinking alcohol, diet, exercise, and stressors in family life or at work or school.

A physical examination comes next. The doctor checks blood pressure, heart rate, and reflexes and tests for tender areas called tender points throughout the body by applying finger pressure or using an instrument called a dolorimeter. A dolorimeter looks like a tube with a spring in it. The physician holds it against an area on the body and slowly increases the pressure. People without fibromyalgia generally report feeling pain when the pressure is over 13 pounds per square inch (6kg/sqcm). Those with fibromyalgia often report pain at a pressure of less than 8.8 pounds per square inch (4kg/sqcm). According to the author of *The Cleveland Clinic Guide to Fibromyalgia*, "4 kilograms is about the pressure it takes to change the color of the nail bed on a person's finger."[15]

In 1990 the American College of Rheumatology established two criteria necessary for a diagnosis of fibromyalgia, and these criteria are still employed today. One criterion is that

Are Tender Points Valid Diagnostic Criteria?

Some doctors have challenged the validity of using tender points in diagnosing fibromyalgia. Some of these experts believe that the number of tender points required for diagnosis is entirely arbitrary, and others question whether tender points actually indicate that a patient has widespread pain. A 2002 study by the German doctors Thomas Schochat and Heiner Raspe found that many people without widespread pain and other symptoms of fibromyalgia have enough tender points to qualify them for a diagnosis of fibromyalgia. "The results suggest that the use of the combination of chronic widespread pain and a certain number of positive tender points as symptoms defining the syndrome 'fibromyalgia' is arbitrary," wrote the researchers.

In a 2009 article in *The Cleveland Clinic Journal of Medicine*, William S. Wilke reported that 19 percent of people with at least eleven tender points do not have fibromyalgia. However, the Symptom Intensity Scale questionnaire correctly distinguished fibromyalgia from other diseases 95 percent of the time. Wilke concluded that the Symptom Intensity Scale and other questionnaires routinely used in diagnosis, along with a physical examination, should carry more weight than tender points in making a diagnosis and that perhaps the tender point criteria should be abandoned entirely.

Thomas Schochat and Heiner Raspe. "Elements of Fibromyalgia in an Open Population." *Rheumatology*, July 7, 2003, p. 834.

the patient reports widespread pain in all four quadrants of the body for at least three months. The other criterion is tenderness in at least eleven of eighteen standardized tender points.

Many patients with fibromyalgia also have firm, painful knots, or nodules known as myofascial trigger points, in their muscles. Pressing on these knots may result in pain spreading to nearby areas. Some doctors suspect that these knots overlap with the tender points used to diagnose fibromyalgia, and some have suggested that myofascial trigger points be established as further diagnostic criteria. However, this has not yet been implemented.

Other Diagnostic Tools

Although criteria beyond widespread pain and tender points are not required for a diagnosis of fibromyalgia, most doctors also rely on the Symptom Intensity Scale questionnaire in making a diagnosis. This questionnaire asks a patient to specify whether or not he or she has pain in nineteen areas of the body, such as the jaw, chest, abdomen, forearms, upper arms, upper and lower legs, hips, back, neck, and shoulders. Patients also rate their fatigue level on a scale of one to ten. Those with a fatigue score greater than six and pain in eight or more specific areas generally qualify as having fibromyalgia.

Many doctors also employ several other questionnaires to determine how severe a patient's fibromyalgia is. The Fibromyalgia Impact Questionnaire rates how often the patient's symptoms prevent him or her from performing certain activities such as climbing stairs, preparing meals, shopping, and working or going to school. It also asks about sleep quality. The Epworth Sleepiness Scale is another rating tool that helps assess a patient's sleep quality, and it also asks questions that help pinpoint whether pain or breathing trouble are causing sleep disturbances. Various questionnaires that rate mood, such as the Mood Disorders Questionnaire, may be helpful in assessing the presence of depression in people with fibromyalgia.

These types of questionnaires, along with tender point assessments, have shown that although males and females with fibromyalgia have similar symptoms, in general, men have fewer tender points and less hypersensitivity to pain than women do. Men are also less likely to have coexisting conditions such as depression and irritable bowel syndrome. However, men with fibromyalgia are just as likely as women to have severe pain, sleep disturbances, and disability. The main difference among the genders is that males do not seem to feel or report pain as soon as women with the same level of pain do.

Before making a definite diagnosis of fibromyalgia in any patient, a doctor will also perform laboratory blood tests to rule out other diseases that could be responsible for the patient's symptoms. Experts hope that someday objective laboratory tests will be available for diagnosing fibromyalgia, since this would make it easier to distinguish fibromyalgia from similar diseases and would enhance the legitimacy of fibromyalgia as a real disease as well. As scientists learn more and more about the causes of fibromyalgia, the feasibility of developing objective, disease-specific laboratory tests grows exponentially.

CHAPTER TWO

What Causes Fibromyalgia?

Doctors are not yet sure exactly what causes fibromyalgia, but they are discovering that complex interactions among abnormalities in the nervous system and muscles, along with genetic and environmental triggers, all play a role. According to the American Fibromyalgia Syndrome Association: "Fibromyalgia means pain in the muscles, ligaments, and tendons—the soft fibrous tissues of the body. Although the muscles hurt everywhere, they are not the only cause of the pain. Instead, the diffuse, body-wide symptoms are greatly magnified by malfunctions in the way the nervous system processes pain."[16] Therefore, understanding the causes of fibromyalgia requires understanding how the muscles and nervous system work.

Muscles Matter

The human body has over 650 muscles. Muscles are made up of bundles of muscle cells. Muscle cells, also known as muscle fibers, have the ability to contract, or shorten, by sliding tiny protein filaments called sarcomeres past each other, thus shortening the length of the filaments. There are two basic types of muscles: striated (also known as skeletal or voluntary) muscles and smooth, or involuntary, muscles. Striated muscles are attached to bones by cordlike tissues called tendons. When striated muscle cells contract and relax, this pulls on the bones and allows voluntary movement. Voluntary muscles are controlled by the cerebral motor cortex and the cerebellum in the brain. When a person decides to move these muscles, the motor cortex sends electrical signals through the spinal cord. When these signals reach the muscles, the muscles contract. The cerebellum coordinates these muscle movements when it receives feedback telling it where and how much a muscle is moving.

Smooth muscles work automatically and allow internal organs such as the blood vessels, heart, stomach, intestines, and bladder to function. Smooth muscles take longer to contract

An illustration of human musculature. Fibromyalgia patients' muscles have a unique texture and feel to them that differ from patients with other disorders.

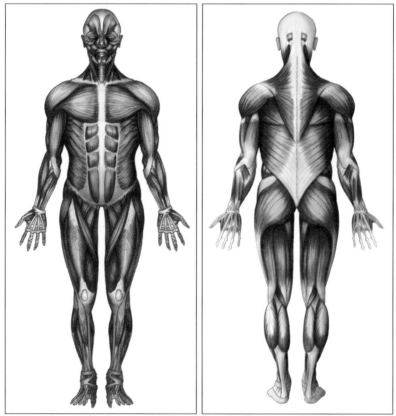

than striated muscles do, but they can contract for longer periods of time because they do not tire easily. Cardiac muscle is a subtype of smooth muscle that controls the heart. Cardiac muscle contractions force blood from the heart to the blood vessels.

Experts do not know whether smooth muscles in people with fibromyalgia have abnormal qualities, but these muscles can hurt just like voluntary muscles can. Skeletal muscles in fibromyalgia patients, though, do have some known abnormal qualities. Explains physical therapist Loren DeVinney in *Fibromyalgia: The Complete Guide from Medical Experts and Patients*: "Fibromyalgia patients' muscles have a unique texture and feel. Their soft tissue (which includes skin, muscle fascia [fibrous tissue that binds other groups of cells together], and tendons) feels different from that of patients who have other injuries or other problems. Normal soft tissue has a soft, pliable texture. Fibromyalgia patients have thicker, stiff tissue that is best described as having a 'gunky' feel to it."[17] Researchers have not yet determined, however, whether these muscle abnormalities are involved in causing fibromyalgia or whether they result from other biochemical events that occur in the disease.

The Nervous System

Evidence that certain abnormalities in the nervous system cause fibromyalgia is much more conclusive than is evidence relating to a causal role for muscle abnormalities. The nervous system comprises billions of nerve cells, or neurons. There are two major types of neurons: sensory and motor. Sensory neurons receive messages from the sense organs and relay these messages to the brain. Motor neurons transmit messages from the brain to the muscles and body organs.

All neurons consist of a cell body and extensions that allow the neuron to communicate with other nerve cells. Small extensions that receive signals from other neurons are called dendrites. Long extensions that transmit signals are called axons or nerve fibers. Axons transmit both chemical and elec-

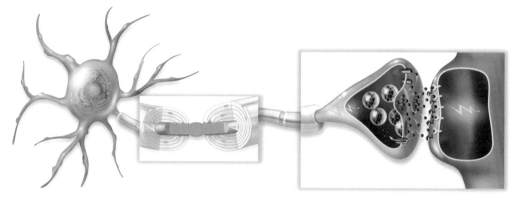

Illustration of a nerve impulse. The dendrite, left, transmits a signal across a nerve fiber to the end of the axon, right, which triggers the release of chemical neurotransmitters from vesicles (tiny balls) across the synapse between nerve cells to gates on a dendrite that leads to the next neuron.

trical signals. When an electrical impulse arrives at the end of an axon, it triggers the release of chemicals called neurotransmitters from vesicles (tiny packets) at the axon's end. These chemicals move across a tiny gap, known as a synapse, between nerve cells. Receptors, or gates, on dendrites in the next neuron take up these neurotransmitters. Some neurotransmitters are excitatory, meaning that they initiate electrical firing and the release of more neurotransmitters in the receiving neuron. Other neurotransmitters are inhibitory; that is, they stop the signal transmission in its tracks. Examples of excitatory neurotransmitters are glutamate, nerve growth factor, and substance P. Serotonin, norepinephrine, and endorphins are examples of inhibitory neurotransmitters.

Neurotransmitters govern every aspect of thoughts, actions, and body functions, including pain. Specialized endings on axons called nociceptors sense and transmit pain signals. Different types and sizes of axons transmit pain signals at different speeds. The thickest axons are called A fibers, and they transmit the fastest signals. A fibers come in four subtypes: alpha, beta, gamma, and delta. Delta fibers are the ones that transmit sharp pain signals. Thinner C axons transmit other types of pain signals, such as burning, aching, or throbbing pain, more slowly than A fibers transmit sharp pain.

As pain or other messages pass from neuron to neuron, this creates pathways, or permanent connections, that remember the messages and relay signals more quickly the next time. Doctors believe that abnormalities in these pathways and in neurotransmitter levels in people with fibromyalgia lead to overactive pain signals becoming wired into certain parts of the nervous system.

Parts of the Nervous System

Neurons are found in the nervous system throughout the body. There are two primary parts of the body-wide nervous system: the central nervous system and the peripheral nervous system. The brain and spinal cord make up the central nervous system. The brain tells the rest of the body what to do. It controls thoughts, memory, sleep, pain, mood, movement, and automatic processes such as heart rate, breathing, and digestion. As well as sending directions to the rest of the body, the brain receives information from neurons in every body part. Different parts of the brain are involved in sending and receiving different types of information.

The brain has three main sections: the forebrain, midbrain, and hindbrain. The forebrain consists of the cerebrum, thalamus, hypothalamus, and pituitary gland. The cerebrum is responsible for intelligence, memory, speech, emotion, and sensation. The outer layer of the cerebrum is known as the cerebral cortex. The cortex receives information from the sensory organs like the eyes, ears, and skin and directs this information to other brain areas for additional processing.

The thalamus helps transmit messages from the sensory organs to the cerebral cortex, and the hypothalamus controls automatic body processes such as digestion, sleep, and heart beat. The hypothalamus also controls the pituitary gland, which releases hormones that govern growth, metabolism, digestion, sexual function, and stress.

The midbrain sits under the middle of the forebrain. The main parts of the midbrain are the tectum, tegmentum, sub-

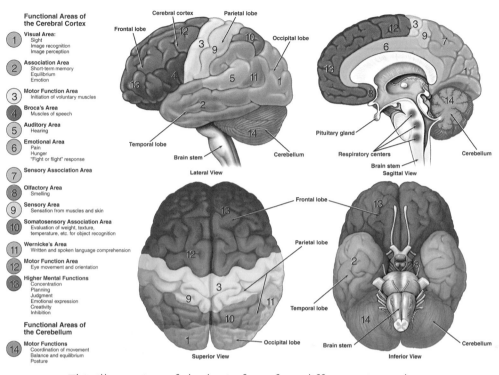

Functional Areas of the Cerebral Cortex

1 **Visual Area:**
Sight
Image recognition
Image perception

2 **Association Area**
Short-term memory
Equilibrium
Emotion

3 **Motor Function Area**
Initiation of voluntary muscles

4 **Broca's Area**
Muscles of speech

5 **Auditory Area**
Hearing

6 **Emotional Area**
Pain
Hunger
"Fight or flight" response

7 **Sensory Association Area**

8 **Olfactory Area**
Smelling

9 **Sensory Area**
Sensation from muscles and skin

10 **Somatosensory Association Area**
Evaluation of weight, texture,
temperature, etc. for object recognition

11 **Wernicke's Area**
Written and spoken language comprehension

12 **Motor Function Area**
Eye movement and orientation

13 **Higher Mental Functions**
Concentration
Planning
Judgment
Emotional expression
Creativity
Inhibition

Functional Areas of the Cerebellum

14 **Motor Functions**
Coordination of movement
Balance and equilibrium
Posture

Cerebral cortex — Parietal lobe — Frontal lobe — Occipital lobe — Temporal lobe — Brain stem — Cerebellum — Pituitary gland — Respiratory centers — Brain stem — Cerebellum — Frontal lobe — Parietal lobe — Temporal lobe — Occipital lobe — Brain stem — Cerebellum

Lateral View — Sagittal View — Superior View — Inferior View

This illustration of the brain from four different views shows the anatomy and functional areas of the forebrain, midbrain, and hindbrain.

stantia nigra, and red nucleus. These parts, along with the pons and medulla in the hindbrain, make up the brain stem, which receives, coordinates, and sends out all of the messages that the brain processes. The brain stem also helps control many of the body's involuntary functions.

The hindbrain is underneath the back part of the cerebrum. It includes the cerebellum, pons, and medulla. The cerebellum controls balance, movement, and muscular coordination.

The other part of the central nervous system, the spinal cord, runs from the base of the brain down the back, inside the spinal bones, or vertebrae. The spinal cord is about 18 inches (46cm) long and contains nerves whose axons extend to every body part.

The Peripheral Nervous System

Axons from nerves in the spinal cord make up the peripheral nervous system, which has two parts: the voluntary part that controls voluntary muscles, and the autonomic, or involuntary part that controls internal organs. The autonomic nervous system, in turn, has two subparts: the sympathetic and parasympathetic nervous systems. The sympathetic nervous system increases heart rate and blood pressure and stimulates blood flow to the muscles, heart, and brain. This prepares the body for the so-called fight or flight response to stress. The parasympathetic nervous system, in contrast, calms down the body's response to stress and stimulation. The functions of all parts of the peripheral, as well as the central nervous system, are controlled by neurotransmitters and nerve firing.

Nervous System Abnormalities in Fibromyalgia

Researchers are uncovering more and more evidence that abnormalities in several parts of the nervous system play a role in causing fibromyalgia. For example, people with fibromyalgia seem to have overactive sympathetic nervous systems and underactive parasympathetic nervous systems. Explains William S. Wilke in *The Cleveland Clinic Guide to Fibromyalgia*: "People with fibromyalgia have higher resting heart rates. When they stand up suddenly after sitting for a while, they may experience an abnormal drop in blood pressure, making them feel light-headed. They may also feel weak during or after a hot bath or shower. This shows that the sympathetic nervous system is overstimulated."[18]

Overstimulation and abnormalities in other parts of the nervous system can cause other symptoms of fibromyalgia, such as central sensitization. People with fibromyalgia appear to have abnormalities in pathways that link the spinal cord to the brain through the brain stem. These abnormalities result from abnormally low levels of the neurotransmitter serotonin.

Genes and Fibromyalgia

Genes are the parts of a deoxyribonucleic acid (DNA) molecule that pass hereditary information from parents to their offspring. Genes reside on chromosomes in the center of each cell. The sequence and chemical composition of genes encode a set of instructions for cell operations.

Genetic traits can either be transmitted directly or as a predisposition, or tendency. An example of a directly transmitted trait is eye color. This trait appears in a baby regardless of environmental or biological events. Some gene mutations (changes in the gene's chemical structure), such as the mutation that causes cystic fibrosis, are transmitted directly.

A genetic predisposition to develop a disease or trait, in contrast, usually results from mutations in multiple genes. Rather than directly causing a disease or other trait to develop, these mutations will not result in a disorder unless certain environmental or biological events also occur. Doctors believe a genetic predisposition makes some people susceptible to developing fibromyalgia.

Without adequate amounts of serotonin, nerve cells fire more than they are supposed to, and signals in these pathways that normally do not reach the brain manage to get through. When this happens repeatedly, the brain essentially becomes rewired to continue to overrespond to incoming pain and sensory signals. Fibromyalgia experts Joseph Meerschaert and Peter Ianni explain in *Fibromyalgia: The Complete Guide from Medical Experts and Patients* how this causes central sensitization: "Being in constant moderate-to-severe pain causes changes in brain activity. Over time, pain signals arriving at the brain from the pain generators elsewhere in the body (i.e., muscles, joints, and nerves) become amplified as ever-larger areas of the brain are aroused by them. [This also] causes amplification of all sensory stimuli—like sounds, visual stimuli, cold, heat, odors, and tastes—not just pain."[19]

Doctors at the National Institute of Dental and Craniofacial Research have found physical evidence of the abnormal brain activity that causes central sensitization. One study used functional magnetic resonance imaging (fMRI) to measure brain activity in people with and without fibromyalgia. fMRI is a special type of MRI that uses magnetic fields and radio waves to see which parts of the brain "light up," or become active, during certain events. The researchers in the study pressed

A magnetic resonance imaging (MRI) scan of a normal human brain. Doctors use MRIs to compare the brain structure in people with and without fibromyalgia.

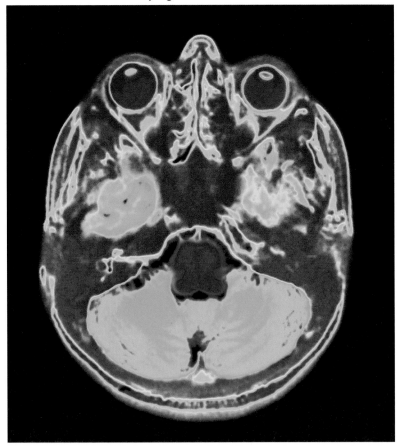

on people's fingernails using 5 pounds per square inch (2.3kg/sqcm) of pressure and asked the individuals to rate the pain on a scale of 0 to 10. At the same time, they measured brain activity with fMRI. People without fibromyalgia typically rated the pain at about a 3. Their fMRIs showed that two brain areas were stimulated during the event. One of these areas was the thalamus, which plays a role in reducing the flow of pain sensations to higher areas of the brain. People with fibromyalgia rated the same pain at about an 8, and their fMRIs showed thirteen brain areas were activated by the pressure. However, these thirteen areas did not include the thalamus. This indicates that more areas of the brain are being activated by pain in people with fibromyalgia and that the thalamus is not doing its job to dampen these pain sensations.

Other studies have shown that fibromyalgia patients show abnormal increases in blood flow to the brain following stimulation to the skin. Doctors have hypothesized, but not yet proved, that this also contributes to ongoing pain and sensitization.

The spinal cord as well as the brain plays a role in causing oversensitivity. In 2003 the Swiss doctor Jules Desmeules and his colleagues found that people with fibromyalgia felt pain in their legs after being given an electric shock that was three times weaker than the shock needed to elicit pain in people without fibromyalgia. The team tracked the pain impulses in the people's nerves and found that these impulses went straight from the site of the shock to the spinal cord. The people reported feeling the shock before the pain impulses ever reached the brain.

Other researchers have determined that abnormally high levels of the neurotransmitters substance P and N-methyl-D-aspartate (NMDA) in the cerebrospinal fluid (the liquid that surrounds the brain and spinal cord) of people with fibromyalgia are responsible for amplifying pain signals in the spinal cord. Substance P is an excitatory neurotransmitter, and the more substance P someone has, the more pain he or she feels. NMDA contributes to this process by boosting the amount of substance P the brain produces.

Sleep Disturbances and Fibromyalgia

Other nervous system abnormalities play a role in causing fibromyalgia symptoms besides oversensitivity. The sleep disturbances that characterize fibromyalgia are not only a symptom of the disease, but also play a role in causing some of these abnormalities.

Doctors have been aware of abnormal sleep biology in people with fibromyalgia for many years. In 1975 Harvey Moldofsky and his associates at the University of Toronto Center for Sleep and Chronobiology in Canada found that alpha brain waves, which normally occur when a person is awake

Monitoring Sleep Stages

Although the body is at rest during sleep, the brain remains active. Doctors can monitor this brain activity with a machine called an electroencephalogram. Electrodes placed on the head pick up brain waves and transmit the information to the electroencephalogram machine, which records the brain waves on paper in graph form.

Different types of brain waves distinguish the different stages of sleep. Sleep has two main phases: REM (rapid eye movement) and non-REM. There are four stages of non-REM sleep. Stages one and two consist of light sleep characterized by electroencephalogram patterns known as theta waves and sleep spindles. Stages three and four involve deep sleep that is also known as slow-wave, or delta wave, sleep. Slow-wave sleep is essential for allowing the mind and body to awaken feeling refreshed and alert.

REM sleep is so named because of the rapid eye movements that occur. Most dreams occur during REM sleep. Electroencephalogram patterns during REM sleep are similar to those while a person is awake; that is, they contain alpha and beta waves. Alpha and relaxed, interrupt deep sleep in people with fibromyalgia. Normally, people only show brain waves called delta waves during deep sleep—not alpha waves. These researchers and others then went on to show that these sleep interruptions contribute to causing fibromyalgia and its other symptoms. "Unrefreshing or nonrestorative sleep are correlated to the myalgia and tender points in FMS. On the rare occasion that sleep is restful, there is substantial improvement in daytime symptoms,"[20] Moldofsky explains.

The manner in which these sleep disruptions cause fibromyalgia is related to neurotransmitters. Interruptions of deep

waves when someone is awake occur during a state of relaxation, while beta waves are present during full wakefulness and alertness.

The five stages of sleep consist of a complete sleep cycle, which lasts ninety to one hundred minutes. A typical sleep cycle consists of stages one, two, three, four, three, two, and REM, in that order. Most people experience four to five sleep cycles per night.

An electroencephalogram monitor shows the electrical activity of a patient's brain during sleep.

sleep lead the brain to produce abnormally low levels of serotonin. Low levels of serotonin, in turn, increase sensitivity to pain and inhibit the ability of naturally produced painkillers called endorphins to diminish pain. Low levels of serotonin can also contribute to the depression and inability to concentrate that often go along with fibromyalgia.

The Root Causes

Scientists believe that the sleep disturbances and other brain abnormalities that cause fibromyalgia are in turn triggered by both genetic and environmental root causes. Evidence that genes play a role comes from studies that show that individuals who are related to someone with fibromyalgia are over eight times more likely than others to develop the disease themselves. Since biologically related family members share similar genes, this means that heredity influences susceptibility to fibromyalgia.

Other studies indicate that certain gene mutations, or changes in genes' chemical structure and sequence, are linked to the disease. Over 30 percent of fibromyalgia patients have a mutation in a gene called the human serotonin transporter gene. This gene determines how much serotonin the brain produces. Since doctors know that serotonin plays a role in causing fibromyalgia, researchers have hypothesized but not proved that human serotonin transporter gene mutations are at least partly responsible for initiating serotonin abnormalities. But other genes also influence the production of serotonin and other neurotransmitters that affect fibromyalgia, so these genes may also have an effect on the process. And not all people with fibromyalgia have human serotonin transporter gene mutations, so other genes are most likely involved.

Research indicates that some of these other genes are likely to be those that govern cell receptors called mu opiate receptors. Mu opiate receptors absorb both naturally produced painkilling opiate endorphins and synthetic opiate-based medications. Studies with laboratory mice have shown that mice that are genetically engineered to lack mu receptors in their

Most Common Factors Patients Perceived as Worsening Fibromyalgia

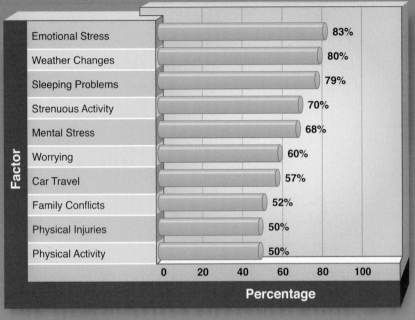

Factor	Percentage
Emotional Stress	83%
Weather Changes	80%
Sleeping Problems	79%
Strenuous Activity	70%
Mental Stress	68%
Worrying	60%
Car Travel	57%
Family Conflicts	52%
Physical Injuries	50%
Physical Activity	50%

Adapted from: NIH, The National Women's Health Center. www.myfibro.com/fibromyalgia-statistics.

brains and spinal cords do not experience normal pain relief from natural and synthetic opiate painkillers. These mice also go on to develop chronic widespread pain that resembles the pain associated with fibromyalgia. Other evidence that mu opiate receptors play a role in causing fibromyalgia comes from positron-emission tomography (PET) imaging scans showing that the brains of many people with fibromyalgia have fewer than normal mu receptors.

Other genes that may be involved in causing fibromyalgia are sex-related genes. Several researchers have proposed that the reason so many more women than men develop fibromyalgia is that females are born with biological traits that make them more likely to experience widespread pain and hypersensitivity in response to stressful events. Studies on rats, for example,

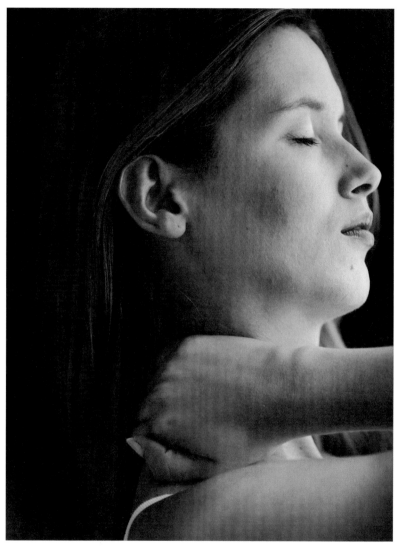

Women suffer from fibromyalgia more than men. Evidence suggests that a combination of social learning and genetic factors may be a contributing factor.

show that females have greater activity in nerve pathways from the peripheral to the central nervous system and produce fewer pain-inhibiting neurotransmitters than males do. Stressful events are also more likely to lead to hypersensitivity to pain in female rats. Investigators believe similar factors may be inborn in humans as well, though they have not yet identified specific genes that underlie these processes.

Studies on people also find evidence of sex-related differences in pain processing. One study found that mu receptors function differently in men and women. When men are exposed to ongoing pain, mu receptors become active and dampen the pain. However, mu receptors become less active when women are exposed to ongoing pain.

Other evidence suggests that a combination of genetics and social learning may contribute to women being more susceptible to developing fibromyalgia than men are. "A family history of pain is associated with increases in pain complaints and enhanced experimental pain sensitivity in females, but not in males,"[21] explains pain expert Roger B. Fillingim of the University of Florida College of Dentistry in a National Fibromyalgia Association article. Fillingim believes this may be due to both inborn gender differences in pain sensitivity and to the fact that women are taught that expressing discomfort is acceptable, whereas most men learn that toughing it out is a desirable masculine trait.

Environmental Factors

Any genetic susceptibility to fibromyalgia, whether associated with sex-linked or other genes, will not result in an individual developing the disease unless other biological or environmental triggers are also present. The most widely studied trigger is stress. The author of *The Cleveland Clinic Guide to Fibromyalgia* explains: "We know that fibromyalgia is a physiological reaction (for some people) to stress. Stress can be external (job or family), environmental (workplace or world), or internal (emotions or physical illness). All types of stress can impair sleep and cause an abnormal production of certain chemicals that control how your nervous system perceives pain."[22]

A study reported in 2007 by fibromyalgia expert Robert M. Bennett and his associates indicated that 73 percent of the fibromyalgia patients they questioned attributed the beginning of their fibromyalgia symptoms to a stressful event such as a serious illness, physical or emotional abuse, a divorce, or a car accident. Other studies have found that many women, in particular, who have fibromyalgia report that they were physically or sexually abused, and some doctors have proposed that abuse can cause fibromyalgia. While no one has proved that abuse or any other specific type of event actually causes fibromyalgia, there is considerable evidence that stressful events in general can launch a cascade of biological malfunctions that lead to the disease.

Doctors know that emotional or physical stress lead the hypothalamus to direct the adrenal glands located above the kidneys to produce excess cortisol. Cortisol is a naturally occurring steroid that, among other things, acts on the brain to decrease the amount of deep sleep. Cortisol also triggers the production of the chemicals epinephrine and norepinephrine, which activate the sympathetic nervous system. When stress persists, cortisol and epinephrine levels remain high, but the amount of norepinephrine starts to decrease to abnormally low levels. Too little norepinephrine, along with deficiencies of serotonin, can then result in nerves becoming hypersensitive to pain.

The sleep disturbances triggered by high levels of cortisol further deplete serotonin levels, and in response the body produces more substance P, which increases the number of pain signals sent from muscles and organs to the brain, as well as heightens pain sensitivity in the spinal cord. Thus, the biochemical abnormalities that characterize fibromyalgia can result from a series of complex interactions between stress, sleep disturbances, genes, and nervous system and muscle biology.

Some experts have proposed that physical trauma, in addition to triggering fibromyalgia via the stress response, can also directly cause fibromyalgia by permanently altering the brain pathways that govern pain. Such experts argue that young people, particularly infants and small children, who are exposed to extreme pain from illness, medical procedures, accidents, or abuse become hypersensitive to pain for the rest of their lives.

Studies have found that many women with fibromyalgia report being sexually or physically abused, leading some doctors to believe abuse can cause fibromyalgia.

Several studies in adults have indicated that people who suffer whiplash injuries to the neck in car accidents are about twenty times more likely to develop fibromyalgia than are those with leg injuries, and this finding has been used as evidence that specific types of physical trauma, rather than generalized stress induced by these injuries, contribute to causing fibromyalgia. Other doctors, however, point out that most people who experience any sort of physical pain or trauma at any age do not go on to develop fibromyalgia, and most fibromyalgia experts have discounted the theory that physical trauma directly causes the disease.

Some authorities claim that doctors, patients, and lawyers who advocate the theory that physical trauma directly causes fibromyalgia do so for the financial gain derived from disability benefits and lawsuits. M. Clement Hall writes in *The Fibromyalgia Controversy*: "The severity of the injury bears no relationship to the prolongation of pain. The factor that seems relevant is the character of the person injured, and their susceptibility to suggestion that they are permanently damaged, are victims of another person's carelessness or of society in general, have a 'right' to be compensated, and will never be able to work again."[23]

Another controversy concerning the possible link between fibromyalgia and physical events involves the disorders neuropathy and thyroid disease. Neuropathy results from nerves degenerating in the limbs, and thyroid disease results from the thyroid gland in the neck producing too much or too little thyroid hormone, which governs metabolism and other body functions related to energy level. Some doctors have proposed that neuropathy and thyroid disease cause fibromyalgia, based on data showing that many people with these disorders end up developing fibromyalgia as well. Thus far, however, there is no proof that either of these diseases has anything to do with causing fibromyalgia.

Complex Interactions

As evidence that fibromyalgia is caused by complex interactions between biochemical, genetic, and environmental factors grows, researchers are striving to put the pieces of the puzzle together in hopes of proving an objective basis for this elusive disease. Such proof will open the door not only to new, objective diagnostic criteria, but also to new treatments that target certain genetic and biochemical abnormalities.

CHAPTER THREE

How Is Fibromyalgia Treated?

Treatment for fibromyalgia depends on the patient's symptoms and severity, as well as on co-occurring disorders such as depression that the patient may have. According to the National Institute of Arthritis and Musculoskeletal and Skin Diseases (NIAMS): "Fibromyalgia can be hard to treat. It's important to find a doctor who is familiar with the disorder and its treatment. . . . Fibromyalgia treatment often requires a team approach. The team may include your doctor, a physical therapist, and possibly other health care providers. A pain or rheumatology clinic can be a good place to get treatment."[24] Physiatrists, or doctors who specialize in physical rehabilitation, and mental health professionals are also commonly part of the treatment team.

The team approach to treatment generally incorporates measures to address underlying causes such as stress and chemical imbalances as well as symptoms of fibromyalgia (FM). These measures may include lifestyle changes to reduce stress and improve sleep quality, diet and exercise modifications, and medications. Fibromyalgia expert M. Clement Hall, who treats many people with fibromyalgia, explains in *The Fibromyalgia Controversy* that "our treatment, our therapy program, is of a person, not a disease, not a set of symptoms, but a person."[25] In such programs, the patient's efforts, along with the physician's recommendations and coordination of treatment team members, are critical in influencing the outcome.

Medications Used in Treatment

Doctors use a variety of medications as one aspect of fibromyalgia treatment. Different drugs or drug combinations work best for different patients, but not everyone is helped by drug therapy.

According to NIAMS: "Perhaps the most useful medications for fibromyalgia are several in the antidepressant class. These drugs work equally well in fibromyalgia patients with and without depression, because antidepressants elevate the levels of certain chemicals in the brain (including serotonin and norepinephrine) that are associated not only with depression, but also with pain and fatigue."[26] There are several types of antidepressants used to treat fibromyalgia. One class of antidepressants is tricyclic antidepressants such as amitriptyline (Elavil). Other types include selective serotonin reuptake inhibitors such as fluoxetine (Prozac) and paroxetine (Paxil), and serotonin-norepinephrine reuptake inhibitors such as duloxetine (Cymbalta) and milnacipran (Savella). These drugs all act to increase levels of serotonin and/or norepinephrine in the brain, and they often help decrease pain as well as improve mood and sleep quality. Other drugs known as serotonin agonists such as alosetron (Lotronex) and serotonin modulators such as trazodone (Desyrel) work in a similar manner. Like any medications, antidepressants can have adverse side effects, such as nausea and dizziness, in some people.

The other most-prescribed drugs for fibromyalgia are the anticonvulsant drugs gabapentin (Neurontin) and pregabalin (Lyrica). Anticonvulsants are usually used to treat epilepsy but are also useful for fibromyalgia because they decrease nerve firing in the central nervous system. Side effects, though, may be serious and may include nausea, constipation, dry mouth, dizziness, tremors, blurred vision, and weight gain.

Muscle relaxants such as cyclobenzaprine (Flexeril) and dopamine agonists such as pramipexole (Mirapex), which increase

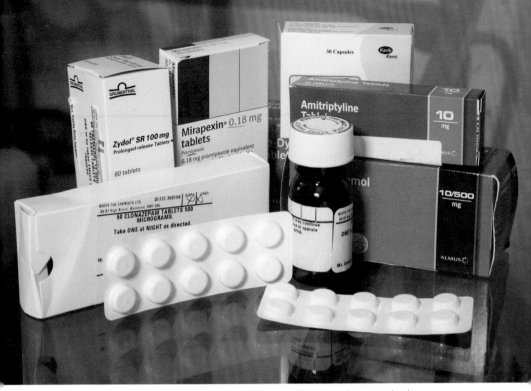

Many medications are used to treat fibromyalgia, including antidepressants, serotonin reuptake inhibitors, and anticonvulsants.

levels of the neurotransmitter dopamine, can also be effective in decreasing pain and improving sleep quality, so doctors sometimes prescribe these drugs for fibromyalgia patients. Dopamine increases the levels of natural painkillers called endorphins.

Some patients benefit from antianxiety drugs like lorazepam (Ativan) or from tranquilizers such as perphenazine (Triavil), and many also need sleep aids such as zolpidem (Ambien). But some sleep aids, such as benzodiazepines, diminish the restorative, slow-wave sleep, so they are not recommended for people with fibromyalgia.

A variety of pain relievers also help some patients. Medications such as acetaminophen (Tylenol) or narcotic painkillers like meperidine (Demerol) or tramadol (Ultram) may be effective. But too much acetaminophen can cause liver damage, and narcotic painkillers can have many adverse side effects and can be addictive, so their use must be carefully monitored. Pain medications that decrease inflammation, such as aspirin, ibuprofen, and naproxen, are not effective in treating

Treating Depression and Fibromyalgia

Because many people with fibromyalgia are also depressed, experts say that most treatment plans must include antidepressant medication and/or psychotherapy to reduce the depression. More and more fibromyalgia experts are realizing that treating coexisting depression is a necessary first step, even before other symptoms of fibromyalgia are addressed. As rheumatologist William S. Wilke explains in *The Cleveland Clinic Guide to Fibromyalgia*:

> When someone has fibromyalgia and depression, we treat the depression first and then the causes of the symptoms of fibromyalgia. It's not because we can't treat fibromyalgia; it's because we don't always have the perfect treatment for depression—and until that's treated, the symptoms of fibromyalgia will continue. . . .
>
> The more severe the depressed mood, the less effective any [fibromyalgia] treatment. This tells us that depression, a cofactor of distress in fibromyalgia, must be addressed in order to make treatment options work.

William S. Wilke. *The Cleveland Clinic Guide to Fibromyalgia*. New York: Kaplan, 2010, pp. 54, 98.

fibromyalgia because the disease does not involve inflammation. In some instances, anti-inflammatory drugs can worsen fibromyalgia.

Approved Drugs

Of all the drugs used to treat fibromyalgia, only three are specifically approved by the U.S. Food and Drug Administration

(FDA) for this purpose. These are pregabalin, duloxetine, and milnacipran. The other drugs doctors prescribe are all approved for use in other disorders, and they help treat certain symptoms in fibromyalgia such as pain or sleep difficulties as well. This is known as off-label usage. Drug manufacturers do not test every drug they market on every possible disease; this would be too costly and time consuming. So if a drug is proved to be safe and effective for treating a symptom in one disease, doctors often prescribe it for the same purpose in other diseases.

Overall, even fibromyalgia patients treated with any of the fibromyalgia-approved drugs do not experience dramatic improvements. "About half of all treated patients seem to experience a 30% reduction of symptoms, suggesting that many patients with fibromyalgia will require additional therapies,"[27] writes University of Florida researcher Roland Staud in the journal *Drugs*.

Injections and Other Invasive Therapies

When oral drugs or drug combinations are not effective, doctors who specialize in pain management can administer injections or employ other invasive pain-management techniques. One procedure involves the physician injecting anesthetics into peripheral nerves to block pain in a specific body area. These injections can provide temporary relief for hours, days, or even weeks. They do have risks, such as bleeding, infection, and damage to the nerve.

Injections of anesthetics directly into the spine can also provide temporary relief of pain in certain body regions, such as the back or the legs. But these injections can cause nerve damage, severe headaches, infections, or bleeding, so, like peripheral nerve injections, they must be performed by a highly skilled doctor.

When repeated nerve injections fail to provide relief, doctors can destroy the endings of the painful nerves using techniques called cryolesioning and radiofrequency lesioning. With cryolesioning, the physician uses an instrument called a cryoprobe to freeze the nerve endings. The cryoprobe tip has a temperature of -94°F (-70°C). This procedure can cut down on pain signals for weeks or months, until the nerve endings regenerate.

Instead of using cold, radiofrequency lesioning applies heat to the nerve endings. The heat permanently destroys these nerve endings but can result in nerve inflammation and pain in other areas of the nerve, so many doctors hesitate to employ this technique. When a patient has ongoing widespread pain that involves many nerves, using cryolesioning or radiofrequency lesioning in multiple areas would be impractical and dangerous as well.

Another option for controlling severe fibromyalgia pain is using electrical stimulation to the spinal cord to block pain signals from being transmitted to the brain. Here a doctor implants an electrical stimulator permanently in the spine, and the patient can remotely activate the device when needed.

A similar technology involves the physician implanting a pump and tubing under the skin and connecting these items to tubing implanted in the spine. When activated, the pump dis-

Spinal injections of anesthetics in fibromyalgia patients can provide temporary relief of pain but may cause nerve damage, severe headaches, and infections.

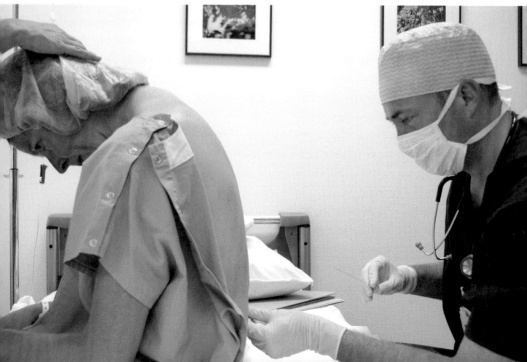

penses pain medication directly into the spinal cord. Possible adverse effects include nerve damage, headache, spinal cord injury, and infection.

As with orally administered drugs, these other methods of administration do not work for all patients. Even when they are effective, any sort of drug treatment is enhanced by other measures that fibromyalgia experts consider to be an essential part of any treatment program.

Nondrug Aspects of Treatment

Other treatment measures consist of various lifestyle adjustments and other efforts on the patient's part to take an active role in maximizing treatment success. One essential element in any treatment program is education. The author of *The Cleveland Clinic Guide to Fibromyalgia* advises patients: "One of the most important things you can do to treat fibromyalgia is to reduce feelings of helplessness. If you know what causes fibromyalgia and what can be done to relieve the symptoms, you are more likely to develop effective strategies to ease your symptoms and respond to treatment."[28]

Education combined with stress-reduction techniques such as meditation and tai chi is especially effective. Studies show that patients who participate in stress-reduction programs and attend education classes or educate themselves using authoritative books, journals, and websites experience greater reductions in pain and improvements in everyday functioning than those who engage only in education or stress reduction exclusively. In addition, combining either one of these practices with medication therapy will often result in more symptom reduction than with using drug therapy alone.

Another lifestyle modification that is often helpful is called sleep hygiene. This consists of measures to complement the effects of sleep medications. One sleep hygiene measure is going to bed and getting up at the same time each day, regardless of fatigue. Other measures include limiting daytime naps to thirty minutes, not eating a large meal within two hours before bedtime, using the bedroom only for sex and sleeping (not for

Education combined with stress-reduction techniques, such as yoga, meditation, and tai chi, have been found to be particularly effective in treating fibromyalgia.

reading or watching TV), avoiding alcohol and caffeine, relaxing with a warm bath before bed, and keeping the bedroom cool and dark.

The Role of Diet

Proper nutrition is also important in fibromyalgia treatment. Some practitioners tout special fibromyalgia diets, but NIAMS states that "although some patients report that they feel better when they eat or avoid certain foods, no specific diet has been proven to influence fibromyalgia."[29] Experts do, however, recommend that people with fibromyalgia eat a healthy, well-balanced diet that enhances overall health. Some nutritional deficiencies can exacerbate pain and disability, and being obese can place stress on the joints and muscles that heightens pain as well. Thus, many fibromyalgia doctors recommend that fibromyalgia patients who do not eat well or who need to lose weight consult a nutritionist who can assess nutritional deficiencies or prescribe a healthy weight-loss diet plan.

Nutritionist Sharon Ostalecki, who wrote the book *Fibromyalgia: The Complete Guide from Medical Experts and Patients*, states in her book that she has seen positive changes in patients, including herself, who begin eating a healthier diet. She says: "During my years as a professional in this field, I have seen patients experience improved energy and concentration, endure less fibro-fog and fatigue, and enjoy improved sleep. My own fibromyalgia symptoms confirm this observation—eating well has significantly enhanced my own well-being."[30]

Ostalecki finds that many people's diets contain insufficient protein and that this can lead to an inability of the body to repair muscle cells. This can exacerbate muscle pain and weakness. She recommends that such patients increase their consumption of protein-rich foods such as fish, eggs, beans, dairy products, and lean meats. Many people also eat too many processed foods that are high in refined sugar and flour. This can lead to rapid spikes in blood sugar levels, which can exacerbate fatigue and mood swings, so Ostalecki often recommends that patients cut down on processed foods.

Exercise and Fibromyalgia

Exercise, as well as diet, is important in fibromyalgia treatment. Many patients, however, have difficulty beginning a regular exercise program because exercise initially worsens fibromyalgia pain. Experts say the key to minimizing the pain that exertion brings about is to start off slowly and gradually increase the amount of exercise to a tolerable level. The American Fibromyalgia Syndrome Association explains: "If you do not exercise on a regular basis, the performance of normal daily living activities will start to cause more pain. Rather than give in to the increased pain sensitivity related to exercise, patients are advised to do mild exercise in short intervals (such as five minutes at a time) to keep the muscles fit while not over-taxing them."[31]

Most fibromyalgia experts recommend that patients work up to doing about thirty minutes of walking, riding a stationary bicycle, swimming, playing tennis, or doing other forms of mild to moderate aerobic exercise at least three times per week. Overly strenuous exercise such as running or weight lifting should usually be avoided. Studies show that regular mild to moderate exercise improves sleep quality and ultimately results in decreased pain levels.

Physical therapists can recommend exercise programs that benefit specific patients, and they can also use muscle stretching techniques and heat and cold applications to the skin to help alleviate pain. Sometimes physical therapists prescribe back or neck braces to support painful areas.

Assessing Treatment Outcome

Whatever forms of treatment a treatment team prescribes, assessing its effectiveness can be challenging, as the author of *The Fibromyalgia Controversy* explains: "Because so much of the range of symptoms in fibromyalgia is subjective, to gain an objective comparison measurement is difficult. If one wishes to know whether the treatment has served its purpose, it's essential to define the symptoms at regular intervals and to make comparative measurements over a period of time."[32]

Doctors employ the same questionnaires they use in diagnosing fibromyalgia to assess improvements in pain, mood, sleep quality, and everyday functioning. Most experts consider an improvement of 30 percent in any one symptom an indication that treatment has been successful.

Patients who show the most improvement are usually those who follow their doctors' advice on taking certain medications, exercising, eating a healthy diet, educating themselves about fibromyalgia, and practicing stress-reduction techniques. But even with improvements, fibromyalgia does not go away, and

Most FM experts recommend that patients work up to doing aerobic exercises, such as walking, swimming, and bike riding, three times a week for about thirty minutes per session.

a treatment program must continue indefinitely and may have to be changed as the patient's condition changes.

Alternative Treatments

Since fibromyalgia treatments do not help all patients, and since the drugs used can have adverse side effects, many patients try alternative therapies, such as herbal supplements, special diets, acupuncture, hypnosis, and others. Alternative treatments are usually not accepted by mainstream doctors, and most are not proven to provide any benefit. Some, besides being ineffective, are even harmful. But some are safe and helpful.

Doctors caution that any alternative therapy that promises a cure, guarantees success, requires an upfront payment, or uses the words "miracle" or "secret" is a hoax that does little more than take a lot of money from unwitting patients. Nutritional supplements and other alternative products are not regulated by the FDA the way drugs and other approved

Ineffective Alternative Treatments

Many alternative therapies have been promoted for alleviating symptoms or even curing fibromyalgia, but most have proved to be ineffective. Below are a few of the popular remedies that reputable doctors say will not help treat fibromyalgia.

Some practitioners claim that hypnotizing patients and leaving them with subconscious suggestions to sleep better or to not feel pain can relieve symptoms of fibromyalgia. However, there is no evidence to support these claims.

Magnetic mattresses and magnetic strips that attach to the body have been touted by their manufacturers to have pain-relieving qualities. However, studies show that these products are no more effective than placebos (fakes that look like the real thing). The FDA has investigated magnetic therapy product manufacturers for making false claims.

Various over-the-counter dietary supplements such as S-adenosylmethionine, Super Malic, dehydroepiandrosterone, melatonin, emu oil, hyaluronic acid, shark cartilage, and glucosamine do nothing to help fibromyalgia.

Cough medicines containing guaifenesin have been widely touted as a cure for fibromyalgia. However, experts say they do not help patients with anything except relieving a cough.

Many alternative therapies for fibromyalgia have been tried, including hypnosis. No scientific evidence supports claims that hypnosis is effective.

therapies are, and people who sell these products often make unfounded and misleading claims. Therapies that are touted by unaccredited "fibromyalgia clinics" advertised on the Internet and in newspapers, magazines, and on television should also be avoided. The author of *The Cleveland Clinic Guide to Fibromyalgia* writes: "If it looks and sounds too good to be true, it generally is."[33]

Some alternative therapies that do not claim to be "cures" and that are administered by licensed professionals do seem to help some people with fibromyalgia and are not harmful. One such therapy is acupuncture. Acupuncture has been proved to alleviate pain and improve sleep quality in disorders other than fibromyalgia, and many people with fibromyalgia report that it helps alleviate their pain and helps them sleep better, even though no scientific studies have proved it to be effective for fibromyalgia. Acupuncture is an ancient Chinese medical practice that involves a doctor inserting fine needles into various points on the skin that correspond to pain sites and organ systems within the body.

Muscle biofeedback is another alternative therapy that is reported to help some patients. Here a therapist places biofeedback sensors over a muscle group, and an electronic machine measures muscle tension and relays this data to the patient via a computer screen. Patients can learn to identify how tense their muscles are, and they can then learn to relax the muscles when they tense up. Studies have shown that this reduces pain and sensitivity in some people.

Some patients claim that electrically stimulating the skin with a transcutaneous electrical nerve stimulation (TENS) unit or a percutaneous electrical nerve stimulation (PENS) machine temporarily relieves pain, but no one has proved that these devices specifically help fibromyalgia patients. A TENS unit consists of a small, battery-operated device that delivers electrical pulses to the skin through surface electrodes. PENS machines are similar, but deliver stimulation under the skin with small needles.

Various massage techniques are popular for pain relief for many conditions, and some people with fibromyalgia claim that gentle massage is effective for them. However, doctors caution that deep, intense massage can worsen pain in people with fibromyalgia.

A therapist inserts acupuncture needles into a fibromyalgia patient to relieve pain. Acupuncture has not been completely accepted by doctors as an effective alternative treatment.

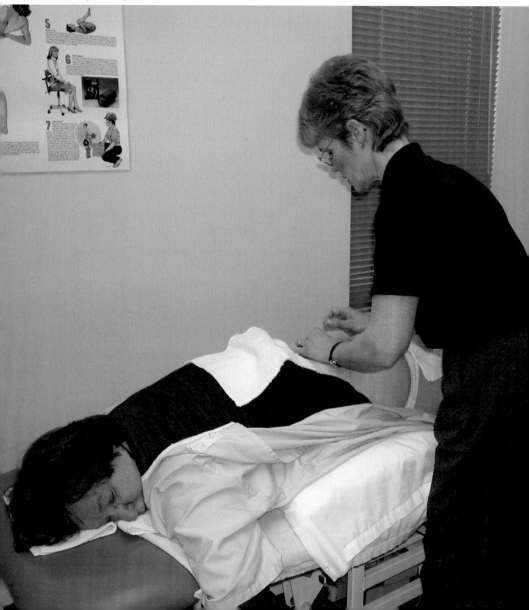

Another therapy that seems to help some people is balneotherapy, in which an individual soaks in a therapeutic bath containing warm water and sulfur or bath salts. Many health spas offer balneotherapy, which is not harmful but seems to provide very limited pain relief for those it does help.

Until doctors develop more effective conventional treatments, patients will continue to try alternative remedies that sound promising in hopes of relieving their symptoms and making life with fibromyalgia easier.

CHAPTER FOUR

Living with Fibromyalgia

Living with fibromyalgia (FM) can be physically and emotionally challenging, especially for patients who have a severe form of the illness that impacts their ability to do everyday things. Any chronic disease brings questions and issues about overall quality of life to the forefront, but when ongoing pain is involved, these issues take on added urgency. Patients often become angry and depressed about the future they face with chronic agony and fatigue that will not go away.

Psychologists report that people diagnosed with chronic diseases typically go through several stages of grieving, because even if the disease is not life threatening, it does result in the loss of the individual's previous lifestyle and identity. These stages may include denial, anger, fear, bargaining with God, depression, and acceptance. Not all patients go through all these phases, and the duration and intensity of each may vary among those who do experience them. Some people become stuck in one phase and never progress to the next. Most people who manage to learn from each stage and to move on to the acceptance phase end up leading the most fulfilling lives.

The Challenges Begin
The stages of grieving and adaptation and the challenges of living with fibromyalgia can begin even before a doctor diagnoses

the disorder. If the diagnostic process takes a long time, this adds to the frustration and coping challenges, as well as delays treatment that can alleviate symptoms.

Bill St. John, an athlete who developed fibromyalgia in his twenties, found the difficulties in obtaining a diagnosis extremely frustrating. He writes:

> On top of the pain, I had to endure repeated misdiagnosis. I was diagnosed with everything from hypertension to arthritis and mixed connective tissue disease. For my family and me this added even greater anxiety to an already stressful situation. . . .

Because firbromyalgia causes the loss of a patient's former lifestyle, FM sufferers go through several stages of grieving. These stages may include anger, fear, and bargaining with God before finally accepting the condition.

The correct diagnosis of fibromyalgia was a real break-through for me. It only took 15 years. It ended the anxiety associated with the many misdiagnoses and gave a name and identity to my nemesis.[34]

A patient named Melissa S. Herman found her diagnosis with fibromyalgia to be a relief for other reasons. "When I was diagnosed with fibromyalgia four years ago, I was so relieved. I didn't have a terminal illness and I wasn't going crazy! Not that it's any fun to have the chronic pain and the symptoms that go along with the condition, but it's much better than what my mind was imagining,"[35] she wrote in a National Fibromyalgia Association article.

Like Herman, many patients find that being told that they are crazy or are imaging their illness is one of the most frustrating and stressful parts of living with fibromyalgia. Irene Leeder, who was not diagnosed for many years after her symptoms began, says that she was frustrated by doctors and other people telling her both before and after her diagnosis that she was complaining about nothing. She writes:

I just wish that fibromyalgia would be respected and that those suffering from it would be respected, the same as someone with diabetes or cancer. . . . For my-self, the very worst part of this is having it sloughed off as being something in my head and getting no help from doctors. It's a very isolating thing to have. . . . We are NOT feeling sorry for ourselves, we are fighting tooth and nail to try and find solutions so we can feel better and lead normal lives.[36]

Everyday Disruptions

Despite the relief that many patients feel upon receiving a diagnosis, the physical and emotional challenges of fibro-myalgia continue on a day-to-day basis and can disrupt every aspect of a person's life. The pain, fatigue, thinking and memory problems, and mood disturbances that go along with

A fibromyalgia patient displays the drugs she uses to treat the disorder. Seventy percent of patients report spending one hundred to five hundred dollars per month on medications alone.

fibromyalgia can make it difficult or impossible for some patients to perform everyday tasks, attend school, or continue to work. One study found that 50 percent of the people with fibromyalgia found it difficult or impossible to climb stairs. Twenty-five percent had trouble standing for five minutes. Some patients must start using a wheelchair. Rebecca Williams, who was extremely active before she developed the disease, was so debilitated that she required a wheelchair to get around. She became socially withdrawn and rarely left her house. Jane Charlton, who developed fibromyalgia at age eighteen, was so exhausted and frustrated by pain and fibro-fog that she stopped driving for a year after realizing that she was lost and could not find her way home from work one day. She also had to stop working. In *Fibromyalgia: The Complete Guide from Medical Experts and Patients*, Charlton writes:

Men and Fibromyalgia Support Groups

Despite the benefits of support groups, some men have diffi-culty joining or becoming active in a support group for a disease that primarily affects women. Tom Hinz, who started and leads a fibromyalgia support group in Wisconsin, remarks in a National Fibromyalgia Association article:

> The biggest challenge that I have found is the lack of males willing to come forward and be a part of the group. Right now, I am the only male that is part of the support group on a regular basis. I know of two men who have fibro-myalgia in the area. One of them was willing to become a member of the group but has not become a regular at the meetings. It's not easy for a guy, especially if he is not particularly comfortable in the circumstances, to come to a support group. I don't have a problem facilitating a group that is all female, other than me. But that is not always an easy thing for males.

Quoted in National Fibromyalgia Association. "Tom Hinz." November 6, 2008. www.fmaware.org/site/News2da17.html?page=NewsArticle&id=7811.

"Before [fibromyalgia] I had always been an active person. I loved to walk, swim, and spend time with family and friends. Now I just existed . . . just getting out of bed was exhausting. My body felt like it was made of cement. I didn't know what to do. I was losing myself to this pain and fatigue and nothing I did seemed to make a difference."[37]

Approximately 20 percent of the fibromyalgia patients in the United States file for disability benefits because they are no longer able to work. About 33 percent of the patients who continue to work report that they must modify their work by shortening their workdays or by changing to jobs that are less physically or mentally demanding.

Not being able to work or having to change jobs can result in decreased income. Even those patients who receive disability payments rarely take in enough money to live comfortably. Doctor visits and treatments for fibromyalgia are expensive even when an individual has medical insurance, and a loss of income or loss of a job can intensify the financial burden on individuals and families. In one study over 70 percent of the patients surveyed reported spending between one hundred and five hundred dollars per month on medications alone.

Special Challenges for Men with Fibromyalgia

Since most fibromyalgia patients are women, and because society in general tends to view males who complain about pain and fatigue as weak and unmasculine, men with the disease may face unique challenges beyond the usual lifestyle and financial disruptions. Robert Leider, a man who developed fibromyalgia after a serious car accident, explained in an article that many men with fibromyalgia suffer in silence and are afraid to tell anyone they have the disease because of this attitude. He says:

> Most of the time we just shut up about it—the pains, the aches, the waves of exhaustion—and just behave badly. We get grumpy with our family, friends, and eventually even our co-workers and bosses. This is a male thing akin to not asking for directions, or waiting until your leg falls off to drag your butt to a doctor. . . . We men are under pressure to provide for our families, to move heavy objects, to participate in sports, to play ball with our kids—to be who we really are. I never told anyone I had fibromyalgia. As a guy I still thought it wasn't cool.[38]

Special Challenges for Kids

Children and teens with fibromyalgia also face unique challenges. Fibromyalgia can affect kids academically and socially.

Jerry Sauve, who developed fibromyalgia at age eight, began missing more and more days of school because of pain, fatigue, and frequent colds and stomach ailments. His parents home-schooled him for a year but decided he should go back to public school when they realized he was not learning very much at home. Sauve was happy to go back to school but became frustrated by the fact that he continued to miss many days of school and by the realization that he was an outsider among his peers. As he explains:

> I fell so far behind that by the time I started something, the rest of the class was finishing it. Whether I went to school hardly mattered, because it was virtually impossible for me to catch up, much less to participate. In addition to this pressure, other factors began to weigh in. First, I couldn't just be one of "them" anymore. . . . Nothing makes you stand out more than being gone for a month or more at a time—while everyone thinks you died or are in the hospital—and then returning out of the blue. There were kids who had actually forgotten about me, that I had to reintroduce myself to. These were kids I'd gone to school with for two years already! Ouch.[39]

Elizabeth Kinzey, who was diagnosed with fibromyalgia when she was in middle school, was teased by classmates. In a National Fibromyalgia Association article, she says: "I got some negative reactions, a lot of jokes and stuff. Most of them were based on ignorance—like 'crybaby' and that kind of stuff. That just made me want to get the message out about what it is: one, that it's not contagious; two, that I'm not dying; and three, there *is* something wrong. It's not that I'm not doing something because I don't want to, or I want to get out of PE class."[40] So Kinzey and a friend gave a talk, performed a song, and handed out information packets about fibromyalgia at a school entertainment event. Both were pleased by the audience's positive and compassionate reactions.

Challenges for the Family

The social and practical challenges presented by fibromyalgia can affect patients of any age, as well as family members. Donna Sellers, whose son was diagnosed with fibromyalgia at age eight, explains how the disease affected her family: "It's a different family lifestyle. We vacation very close to home. We don't take long trips or spend the day at places like Disneyland as many families do. We plan activities and trips that will bring success instead of pain and frustration. We all had to learn to

Experts point out that, while it is important for families and caregivers to provide support for a loved one with FM, it is essential that caregivers take care of themselves and continue to do things they enjoy.

s-l-o-w down and do things that would be successful for Collin, making for a good day/trip for the whole family."[41]

When a person with fibromyalgia cannot perform everyday tasks, other family members must be responsible for helping out and for doing things such as bathing and dressing the individual if necessary. This may mean that a spouse or parent must stop working to be a full-time caregiver, or that older children must assist a parent or sibling. As Brianna Tulin, a teen whose mother has fibromyalgia, found out, this made her own life challenging. But Tulin believed that doing all she could to help was important. In a National Fibromyalgia Association article, she encourages other teens in similar situations to do their part as well:

> I think kids that have parents with a bad illness should learn as much as they can about the disease so they know what's going on better and how to deal with it. Also, really try to help out with things at home as much as possible. I have to help my mom get around, get her things when she needs them and just be available when she needs my help. It isn't easy, but I try really hard to be patient with her and other kids with sick parents should too.[42]

Experts point out that while it is important for families and caregivers to accomodate and help out loved ones with fibromyalgia, it is also essential that caregivers take care of themselves and continue doing things they enjoy, even if the patient cannot always participate. In an article titled "How to Be a Better Friend, Spouse, or Relative to Someone with FM," psychologist John Fry advises family members not to forget about their own needs:

> Research has shown that spouses of those with FM have an increased risk of [social] withdrawal, a weakened immune system, deterioration in physical health, discouragement, worry, and loneliness. Twenty-five percent of spouses are diagnosably depressed. These issues can all be countered, but it requires extra attention to self care. . . . Continue doing enjoyable activities and keep other friendships going.[43]

Methods of Coping

Experts say that other coping strategies can also help patients and family members live as fully as possible with fibromyalgia. The key to making these strategies work is accepting the limitations imposed by the disease while striving to control those aspects of life that are controllable. Kristine Creamer-Pardieu, for example, learned that accepting her need to rest frequently and even to spend most of a bad day resting helped reduce her resentment of fibromyalgia. As she writes: "Some days I just 'putz' around the house if 'putzing' is all I can do. It is difficult on those days, as my mind wants me to be active, but my body just can't do it. I have had to forgive my body for that, and to learn to go with the flow."[44]

Melissa Olivadoti, who was diagnosed with fibromyalgia at age eighteen, found that educating herself about the disease at a pain center where she went for treatment helped her cope and learn to pace herself to enhance the quality of her life. Olivadoti writes: "After many talks with those at the center, I realized that, while I had a condition that would give me good and bad days, I could still maximize the good and minimize the bad while striving toward my goals. I made myself a promise to respect my body, but not let it stop me from my goals."[45]

People who must change careers because of fibromyalgia find that accepting the need to do so and making the best of the situation can open doors they never imagined possible. Melvin Fromm, Jr., for example, was planning to work as a Hollywood stuntman, but this became impossible when he developed fibromyalgia. But he discovered that he had another talent—writing songs—when he composed a song for his future wife. He became a country music songwriter whose songs have been aired throughout the world, and he found that his new career helped him cope with the ups and downs of fibromyalgia by allowing him to express his feelings through music and lyrics.

Rebecca Williams, who worked as an interpreter for the deaf, became so debilitated by fibromyalgia that she had to use a wheelchair to get around and had to quit her job because it was too demanding and tiring. She became socially withdrawn until she adopted a service dog to help her out. The dog gave her the courage to train for a new career as a rehabilitation counselor, and she went on to become a part-time service dog trainer so she could help others with disabilities reap the benefits of having a canine companion.

Nicole Sloan, a teacher, did not have to change careers but did require special accommodations because of her fibromyalgia. She arranged to teach classes that were all on the same

Coping Strategies

Doctors at the Mayo Clinic recommend that fibromyalgia patients take several steps to help them cope with the pain and fatigue that go along with the disease:

- Coping strategies for getting through a bad day can range from taking frequent rest breaks throughout the day to watching a funny movie or talking with a favorite friend on the phone. Preparing a list of these strategies in advance can help lessen the impact of fibromyalgia pain.

- Avoid negative self-talk. Studies have shown that what we say to ourselves inside our heads can affect our perception of pain. Turning negative thoughts into positive ones takes practice but is worth the effort.
  Negative: I can't do anything because of my symptoms.
  Positive: I can do many things. I just need to pace myself and take breaks.

- Tell someone when you're having a difficult day.

- Spend your energy "pennies" wisely. Sometimes it helps to think of the amount of energy you have as pennies in a piggy bank. You need to prioritize tasks so that you won't run out of pennies before the day is done.

floor to avoid having to go up and down stairs, and she made sure she took her allotted morning, lunch, and afternoon breaks no matter how busy she was. Sloan also learned to prioritize her activities at home so she had the energy to do what was really important to her. In a National Fibromyalgia Association article, she advises other fibromyalgia patients to do the same: "What is important to you as far as your relationship with your kids? If it's reading them books at night, then make

- Ask for help when you need it. Make a list of people who can help you on bad days.

- Relax with deep breathing exercises, progressive muscle relaxation, and meditation.

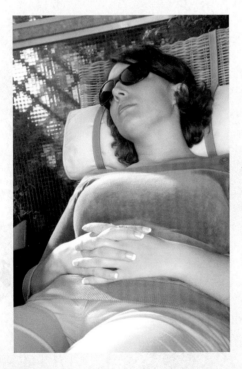

The Mayo Clinic recommends that FM patients take several steps to help them cope. Taking frequent rest breaks, avoiding negative self-talk, doing relaxation exercises, and talking with someone will help them get through the day.

Mayo Clinic. "Fibromyalgia Pain: Options for Coping." www.mayoclinic.com/print/fibromyalgia-pain/AR00055/Method=print.

sure that gets in. I may not be able to pack lunch; I might have to send them [to school] with lunch money. But packing lunch isn't my priority, reading books at night is."[46]

Additional Coping Strategies

Other patients find a variety of other coping strategies to be important in helping them live a full life with fibromyalgia. One important tactic is consulting caring, knowledgeable doctors who are willing to listen to a patient's problems and needs and to partner with the patient to find the best possible treatment plan. Experts say that national fibromyalgia support organizations, local support groups, and local medical societies can give referrals to appropriate doctors and other treatment team members. Once a patient finds health-care professionals with whom he or she is comfortable, ongoing communication and mutual respect are important in influencing how effectively the individual manages the illness.

Many patients find that consulting a psychologist who specializes in treating people with chronic pain can enhance the effectiveness of any treatment plan devised by other medical team members. A pain psychologist helped Jane Charlton, who had to stop working and was too tired even to take a shower on many days, learn to pace herself to do chores so she would not become overwhelmed by fatigue. The therapist also taught Charlton to be aware of pain signals that indicated she should slow down and rest before the pain became overwhelming, and he helped her change her priorities to alleviate some of the emotional stress that resulted from her resentment of her physical limitations. Rather than mentally beating herself up because she was too tired to clean the house, she learned to accept the fact that the cleaning could wait or that she could ask a family member to help out. Along with benefiting from a tolerable exercise program designed by a physical therapist and taking pain and sleep medications prescribed by her medical doctor, Charlton found that adding the pain psychologist to her treatment team greatly enhanced the quality of her life.

Support Groups and Advocacy

Many patients find that joining a local or online fibromyalgia support group helps them cope as well. According to the National Fibromyalgia Association, "Participation in support groups can provide an opportunity to reach out to others who have had similar challenges and foster an improved understanding of lifestyle management."[47] Some local support groups have informal discussion groups, while others may also sponsor educational seminars or lectures by medical professionals.

Jennifer Herman, who has fibromyalgia and was initially hesitant about joining a support group because she wondered if being with chronically ill people would be depressing, found the opposite to be true. In an article titled "In This Together," Herman writes:

> If you find the right group, it can be a place to get information, receive empathy, find inspiration, and give encouragement. . . .

> Sometimes I feel that "normal" people cannot understand the frustrations that come from having a chronic illness. Support groups help because at the meetings there are others who have the same feelings. The people in the group can listen in a different way. They listen from a standpoint of having been there. My support group friends can acknowledge what I say and then help me see it is possible to work through frustration, hurt, anger, and anything else I am facing. . . .

> Support groups offer people a chance to give to others. . . .

> It is not unusual to attend a meeting and find that someone needs encouragement or a solution to a problem. By reaching out to that person, I turn my focus from myself to someone else. I forget about my own pain as I try to find a way to encourage my friend.[48]

Participating in advocacy efforts, as well as in support groups, can help give people with fibromyalgia a sense of purpose and enhance their coping skills. Many patients join nonprofit organizations such as the National Fibromyalgia Association and participate in events such as fibromyalgia awareness walks, seminars, and speaking to government officials about the need for fibromyalgia education and research. An eleven-year-old boy named Noah Carrillo, who raised over two thousand dollars by walking in a 2010 Fibromyalgia Awareness Means Everything event, stated in a National Fibromyalgia Association article that he found his efforts extremely rewarding: "Even though I was in a lot of pain at the end of that day, it was worth it! I met one other kid with fibromyalgia, and I'm excited to help the NFA [National Fibromyalgia Association] tell as many people and kids as we can about this illness."[49] Added his mother, Maria, "Awareness Day helped Noah feel that he does have a purpose."[50]

Brianna Tulin, a teen whose mother has fibromyalgia, designed a school project about the disease and testified before the Connecticut State Legislature to encourage support for

Participation in fibromyalgia support groups can give people with FM a sense of purpose and enhance their coping skills.

a bill recognizing Fibromyalgia Awareness Day. She speaks about her experience in a National Fibromyalgia Association article: "I was very nervous about meeting our senator but he was very nice and made me feel like I was doing something really good for my mother and millions of others."[51]

These types of advocacy efforts have done much to enhance public awareness and to promote research about fibromyalgia. However, the disease continues to make life challenging for millions of patients and their families, and advocacy groups are pushing for even more education and research to brighten the outlook for those who are affected.

CHAPTER FIVE

The Future

Patients and medical experts recognize the need for improvements in awareness, understanding, diagnosis, and treatment of fibromyalgia in the future. Researchers have a long way to go before they fully understand the causes of the disease, and current treatments are ineffective for many patients. Doctors have no objective methods of diagnosis or of predicting and gauging treatment success. The general public, along with many medical professionals, is still largely ignorant about fibromyalgia (FM) and holds misconceptions that contribute to controversies over its legitimacy as a "real" disease. A patient named Jeff, who was eventually diagnosed with fibromyalgia after experiencing symptoms for two years, aptly expressed this ignorance when he remarked in a National Fibromyalgia Association article, "I knew little about FM at that time, other than it was some woman's disease that was supposed to be in their heads."[52]

Experts point out that in addition to affecting patients, fibromyalgia also impacts society. "The cost of fibromyalgia to both the individual and society is extensive. . . . Prominent fibromyalgia researchers and specialists estimate the costs in the U.S. between $12–14 billion each year and accounts for a loss of 1–2% of the nation's overall productivity,"[53] explains the National Fibromyalgia Association.

Thus, advocacy organizations and researchers are engaged in ongoing efforts to improve education, diagnosis, treatment, and understanding the causes of fibromyalgia to diminish its personal and societal burden in the future. Although much remains to be done, progress on all these fronts has been achieved. May 12 is now dedicated as the annual National Fibromyalgia Awareness Day, and each year on that day advocates hold rallies, walks, educational seminars, and appeals to lawmakers for increased research funding. Similar activities continue throughout the year, and organizations like the National Fibromyalgia Association have also set up ongoing doctor education and support group leader training programs throughout the country. Progress is also being made in all aspects of fibromyalgia research. According to the National Fibromyalgia Association, "In 1990 there were approximately 200 published papers on fibromyalgia studies. Today there are more than 4,000 published reports."[54]

Research on improving diagnosis, treatment, and understanding of the causes of fibromyalgia continues at an unprecedented pace as awareness of the magnitude of the fibromyalgia problem grows.

A doctor checks trigger points on a fibromyalgia patient. Advocacy groups and researchers are engaged in ongoing efforts to improve education, diagnosis, treatment, and understanding of the causes of FM.

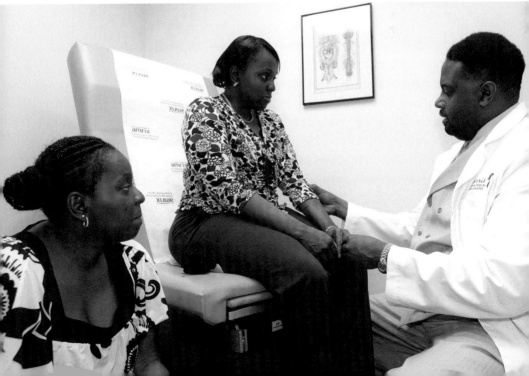

The PROMIS Program

Since one major problem in assessing treatment success in fibromyalgia and many other diseases is that reports of improvements in symptoms are subjective, National Institute of Arthritis and Musculoskeletal and Skin Diseases (NIAMS) is investigating a new program called the Patient-Reported Outcomes Measurement Information System (PROMIS) that it believes will benefit fibromyalgia patients. "The goal of this initiative is to improve the reporting and quantification of changes in PROs [patient-reported outcomes],"[1] explains NIAMS.

Scientists are developing standardized measurements for qualities like pain, fatigue, depression, sleep habits, and social participation, and they hope to use these measurements for objectively quantifying treatment outcome in many diseases. They are incorporating these measurements into a computer program that allows doctors to assess objectively how well treatment is working.

An article on MSNBC.com explains how PROMIS can help doctors and patients:

> PROMIS provides a common language for researchers studying the causes of physical pain and its symptoms. In the past, groups of scientists would use different sets of questions to quantify a patient's physical suffering, making it difficult to compare results. With the push for health care reform, it's becoming more important to show in multiple studies that a therapy works. As a result, more than 1,000 researchers have signed up to try out the new tool.[2]

1. National Institute of Arthritis and Musculoskeletal and Skin Diseases. "Fibromyalgia." www.niams.nih.gov/Health_Info/Fibromyalgia/default.asp.
2. Linda Carroll. "Owie! Hundreds of Ways to Say 'It Hurts.' New Tool Helps Doctors Understand the Pain You're In." MSNBC.com, August 12, 2009. www.msnbc.msn.com/id/32373248/ns/health-health_care.

Research into Improving Diagnosis

The lack of objective diagnostic markers contributes to the controversy over fibromyalgia's legitimacy and results in long delays in diagnosis for many patients. Thus, scientists are seeking to develop more objective diagnostic methods. One study at Beth Israel Deaconess Medical Center in Boston is investigating the use of a technology called a sleep spectrogram to diagnose fibromyalgia. A sleep spectrogram is a chart that specifies how well the heart, lungs, and nervous system are coordinated during sleep. It is generated by an electrocardiogram machine that measures heart function and breathing patterns. The Beth Israel researchers believe that electrocardiogram data, along with blood pressure measurements, can give clues about how heart rhythm and breathing problems may be contributing to the sleep disturbances in people with fibromyalgia.

Previous studies using electroencephalogram machines, which measure electrical activity within the brain, indicate that people with fibromyalgia have abnormalities in brain waves during sleep, but the researchers in the current study believe that using electrocardiogram and blood pressure measurements provides a more accessible method of assessing sleep disturbances. Patients must sleep in a sleep clinic with electrodes attached to their heads to obtain electroencephalogram readings, but people can use an electrocardiogram monitor strapped around the chest and a blood pressure monitor placed around a finger at home, and the data can then be brought to a doctor for analysis.

Researcher Robert J. Thomas explains in an American Fibromyalgia Syndrome Association article that he and his colleagues hypothesize that the sleep disruptions experienced by people with fibromyalgia prevent their blood pressure from dipping normally while they are asleep, and that this quality, along with a sleep spectrogram, may prove to be useful diagnostic indicators. Thomas says:

> We propose to show that FMS patients [fibromyalgia sufferers] are non-dippers—their BP [blood pressure] will

remain increased during sleep because sleep itself is disturbed. The combination of the [electrocardiogram]-based sleep spectrogram and simultaneously measured continuous BP could provide a useful marker of FMS. . . .

The absence of reliable markers of abnormal physiology in FMS has presented a major challenge that we hope to overcome. Sleep then becomes a window that allows clinicians and researchers to look into and track the disease state of FMS.[55]

In another project, researchers at Tel Aviv Sourasky Medical Center in Israel are testing a new sleep-related technology called peripheral artery tonometry. This technology uses a device called the Watch-PATTM100, which employs a probe attached to a patient's finger to measure oxygen levels, heart rate, and breathing changes during sleep. The investigators plan to compare breathing disturbances in fibromyalgia patients and healthy control subjects to see whether breathing problems play a role in the sleep interruptions that occur in fibromyalgia. If this proves to be the case consistently among fibromyalgia patients, this technology could possibly be used in diagnosis.

The research on new diagnostic techniques may also yield insight into some of the mechanisms that cause fibromyalgia, and other studies are investigating causative factors as well.

Research into Causes

Teams of researchers in Spain and Denmark recently found that all the fibromyalgia patients they evaluated had firm nodules in their muscles, while none of the people in a group of healthy control subjects had these nodules. The investigators call the nodules myofascial trigger points (MTPs), and they discovered that MTPs contribute to patients' hypersensitivity to pain. They believe that overactivity in the sympathetic nervous system may be at least partly responsible for the formation of MTPs and are now studying whether deactivating the MTPs will decrease sympathetic nervous system activity and relieve

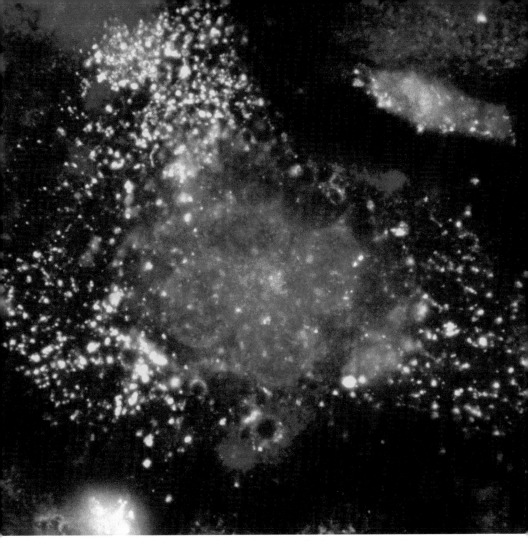

An immunofluorescent light micrograph shows macrophages, a type of white blood cell, producing cytokine proteins. Cytokines are chemical messengers for the immune system, and scientists suspect the immune system plays a role in fibromyalgia.

pain. They are inserting acupuncture needles into the MTPs to cause the nodules to relax and hopefully to release chemicals such as substance P. One of the researchers explains in an American Fibromyalgia Syndrome Association article that "an important question to answer is: which came first, the MTPs or the sympathetic hyperactivity in people with FMS? If deactivating trigger points leads to decreased sympathetic activity, then it will prove that MTPs are one of the causes of sympathetic hyperactivity in FMS."[56]

Research at NIAMS is looking at another possible cause of fibromyalgia—chemical messengers in the immune system called cytokines. Although fibromyalgia does not involve the inflammation that characterizes many immune system disorders, some scientists suspect that the immune system may nonetheless play a role in fibromyalgia. Studies indicate that abnormal levels of certain cytokines lead to fatigue and pain, and other studies show that some cytokines can increase the amount of substance P in the nervous system. No one knows, however, whether the activity of these cytokines causes or results from fibromyalgia, since sleep deprivation can lead to elevated cytokine levels. The researchers are attempting to sort out these questions and to explore other mechanisms by which immune cells may influence chronic pain.

Other research on causes is focusing on genetic abnormalities that may underlie fibromyalgia. Researchers at the University of Sherbrooke in Canada are investigating how genetic mutations that influence the neurotransmitter dopamine may play a role. Dopamine causes the nervous system to release endorphins that reduce pain. Previous studies indicate that the brains of people who do not have fibromyalgia increase the production of dopamine in response to a painful stimulus, but the brains of people with fibromyalgia do not do this. The researchers are now studying the role of a gene mutation called the Ser9Gly polymorphism in this process. People with this mutation require more dopamine than is normally required to stimulate the release of endorphins. "FMS patients already have signs of abnormal pain processing in the spinal cord (e.g. elevated pain transmitters like substance P and glutamate), so having genes that make things worse will have more of an impact on pain thresholds,"[57] explains the American Fibromyalgia Syndrome Association.

NIAMS is also conducting research on genetic causes. One study is investigating abnormalities in a gene called ADRA1A. This gene is associated with adrenaline receptors in the sympathetic nervous system. A 2009 study reported in the journal *Arthritis and Rheumatism* found that mutations in ADRA1A may increase the risk of a person developing fibromyalgia, and that different mutations in the gene affected different symptoms such as morning stiffness, fatigue, and hypersensitivity. The current study is attempting to further understand how the gene works and to clarify exactly how it influences fibromyalgia.

Other NIAMS research is studying identical twins (who have identical genes) and fraternal twins (who do not have identical genes) to assess the relative contributions of heredity and environment to the development of fibromyalgia. The researchers are looking at twins who both have chronic widespread pain, twins where one of them has chronic pain and the other does not, and twins where neither has chronic pain to shed light on this issue.

Research into Behavioral Therapies

As scientists understand more and more about the causes of fibromyalgia, this opens the door to new and improved medical and behavioral treatments. Research on behavioral treatments is centering on weight management, exercise, and stress reduction.

Many people with fibromyalgia are overweight, so researchers at the University of Utah are assessing the effectiveness of a motivational education program in helping overweight patients change their eating habits. The researchers write:

> Research has shown that weight problems are very common in fibromyalgia, and that overweight patients experience more severe pain, disability, and sleep problems than others. Research also suggests that overweight and obesity may contribute to worsening of fibromyalgia symptoms and biochemical vulnerability associated with fibromyalgia. Effective weight management may be important in not only improving general health but also better management of fibromyalgia symptoms.[58]

Since doctors know that regular exercise can also improve symptoms of fibromyalgia, a NIAMS-supported study aims

Overweight fibromyalgia patients experience more severe pain, disability, and sleep problems than other FM patients.

to determine whether increasing general physical activity levels, such as walking up stairs instead of riding in an elevator, can also help. Preliminary results indicate that patients who increase their overall level of physical activity by thirty minutes most days of the week report less pain and disability than those who do not. However, the researchers reported that they were having difficulties motivating people to continue their efforts to be more active, even after the patients saw that they improved from such efforts. Further research is under way to develop methods of helping motivate patients to stay active.

In research on stress management, a study at Wayne State University in Detroit is testing the effectiveness of a new stress-resolution program in reducing fibromyalgia symptoms, compared to a cognitive behavior and fibromyalgia education program. The stress-resolution program, known as Emotional Exposure Therapy, trains patients to focus on their emotions and to develop assertive behaviors, as well as how to practice role-playing and sharing their feelings with others. The investigators are asking patients in the study to rate their pain, fatigue, sleep quality, depression, anxiety, satisfaction with life, and ability to perform everyday tasks both before and after each program.

Research on Medications

Improving treatment outcomes through new and better medications is another focus of treatment research. Scientists develop new drugs in a laboratory and initially test a compound on laboratory animals for safety and effectiveness. Then clinical trials on human volunteers may begin, and if the drug's therapeutic value is proved to outweigh any adverse side effects, the Food and Drug Administration (FDA) may approve the drug for sale. Doctors also conduct clinical trials to test drugs that are already approved for use in other diseases.

Since researchers perform most clinical trials on adult volunteers, many drugs gain approval for use in adults, but not in children. The FDA requires additional testing to assess appropriate doses, safety, and effectiveness in people under age eighteen. Doctors are currently testing the drug duloxetine, an antidepressant approved for use in adults with fibromyalgia, on children and adolescents with the disease.

An experimental drug now being tested on adults with fibromyalgia is neurotropin. Scientists make neurotropin by combining inflamed rabbit skin and vaccinia virus, which is a virus that was once used in smallpox vaccinations. Experts believe neurotropin works to alleviate pain by stimulating serotonin and norepinephrine pathways in the brain. The drug is currently approved to treat fibromyalgia and other pain disorders in Japan but not in the United States.

Drugs already approved in the United States to treat diseases other than fibromyalgia are being tested on fibromyalgia patients as well. A study at East Tennessee State University Research Foundation is testing whether quetiapine (Seroquel XR), which is presently approved to treat schizophrenia, bipolar disorder, and depression, is effective in alleviating pain and sleep disturbances in fibromyalgia patients who are not helped by other medications. Quetiapine can have serious side effects, such as stomach pain, weight gain, dizziness, headache, diabetes, and seizures, so if it proves to be effective in treating fibromyalgia, it would only be used in cases where less dangerous medications did not work.

A Controversial New Drug for Fibromyalgia

Some doctors believe that a drug already used to treat the sleep disorder narcolepsy has great potential for helping fibromyalgia patients. The drug, called sodium oxybate (Xyrem), helps people attain stage three and four sleep. However, the drug has a serious potential for abuse and addiction, and it may have serious side effects such as breathing problems, hallucinations, confusion, nausea and vomiting, blurred vision, and others, so doctors must carefully monitor patients who use it.

Jazz Pharmaceuticals, which manufactures Xyrem, applied to the FDA to approve the drug for treatment of fibromyalgia, based on clinical trials showing that it significantly improved patients' symptoms. However, the FDA turned down the application in October 2010 because of concerns about safety and abuse potential. The National Fibromyalgia Association (NFA) and numerous doctors expressed their support for approving sodium oxybate and have indicated that they hope the FDA will reconsider its decision in the future. States an NFA article:

> Research shows that fibromyalgia patients do not exhibit addiction tendencies. On the contrary, fibromyalgia patients are conservative in their use of pain medications.

> Understandably, the NFA was very disappointed in the panel's vote to presently deny approval of Xyrem for the

A form of thyroid hormone called T3, presently used to treat hypothyroidism, is also being tested on fibromyalgia patients. The deficiency of thyroid hormone seen in people with hypothyroidism leads to a lack of energy, weight gain, sensitivity to cold, and other symptoms, and some doctors believe that low thyroid levels may contribute to symptoms of fibromyalgia

treatment of fibromyalgia. Fibromyalgia patients have the right to have medications available for treatment that have great potential, as shown by in-depth clinical studies, to beneficially impact their quality of life.

Despite this current setback, we will continue to encourage and support Jazz Pharmaceuticals as they go forward to develop further safety precautions that will satisfy the FDA and lead to an approval of this important and effective drug at a future date.

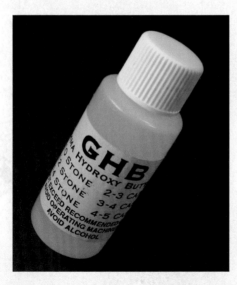

Xyrem is a GHB drug that was designed to help FM patients sleep better. The Food and Drug Adminstration turned down the manufacturer's application because of concerns about safety and the potential for abuse.

National Fibromyalgia Association. "National Fibromyalgia Association Makes Call to Action in Response to FDA Postponement of Decision to Approve Sodium Oxybate (Xyrem) for Treatment of Fibromyalgia." www.fmaware.org/site/News21158 .html?page=NewsArticle&id=9697.

in some people. Researchers at Stanford University are testing thyroid levels in the blood of fibromyalgia patients to see
which individuals have low thyroid levels, and are then administering T3 to those who do to see if it alleviates fibromyalgia
symptoms.

How Do Approved Drugs to Treat Fibromyalgia Work?

In addition to testing new drugs to treat fibromyalgia, researchers are also trying to figure out exactly how drugs already approved to treat the disease work. For example, doctors know
that milnacipran is often effective in reducing pain, but they do
not know whether it works on both the central and peripheral
nervous systems. A team at the University of California at San
Diego is assessing how milnacipran changes levels of serotonin, norepinephrine, and substance P in both the cerebrospinal fluid and blood of patients to determine its mechanism
of action. Tests on cerebrospinal fluid reveal central nervous
system activity, while blood tests indicate what is going on in
the peripheral nervous system.

Another study is investigating whether milnacipran lowers
brain levels of a chemical called ventricular lactate. Scientists
at Beth Israel Medical Center in New York are using an imaging
technique called magnetic spectroscopy, which allows doctors
to measure levels of chemicals in the brain, to measure ventricular lactate levels before and after fibromyalgia patients take milnacipran. The researchers believe that abnormally high levels of
ventricular lactate may contribute to fibro-fog and fatigue, and
they hypothesize that milnacipran may be effective in treating
these symptoms because it lowers brain levels of this chemical.

Researchers at the Cleveland Clinic are investigating another question about milnacipran: Does it improve sleep quality in people with fibromyalgia? Doctors know the medication
improves other symptoms but as yet are unsure of whether it
improves sleep. The Cleveland Clinic researchers are testing
patients' brain waves during sleep with electroencephalo-
grams to find out.

Investigators at Albany Medical College in New York are studying another approved drug, duloxetine, to shed light on why it helps some, but not all, people with fibromyalgia. The researchers are performing skin biopsies, which involve cutting out a small piece of skin and examining it under a microscope, on patients to evaluate whether certain nerve and blood vessel characteristics present in the skin correlate with whether or not an individual experiences pain relief from duloxetine. Previous studies have indicated that some people with fibromyalgia have abnormalities in nerve endings on the ends of small blood vessels, and the investigators are attempting to find out if this affects people's response to medication.

Drugs like Cymbalta contain the drug duloxetine, an antidepressant. Duloxetine helps some FM patients, but not all.

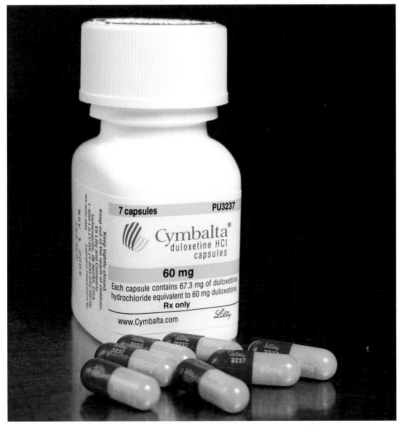

Research on Nondrug Treatments

In addition to studying new and existing drug treatments, researchers are also exploring nondrug therapies for fibromyalgia. One alternative therapy that appears to help many patients is acupuncture, and several researchers are conducting scientific studies to find out if it is truly effective. They are administering acupuncture treatments to groups of patients in an experimental group and sham treatments that actually do nothing to patients in control groups to assess whether the treatments themselves, rather than the expectation of success, are leading to improvements in pain. A team at the University of Michigan is taking this research a step further and is assessing whether acupuncture treatments work by changing activity in certain brain areas. The researchers are using MRI (magnetic resonance imaging) and PET (positron-emission tomography) imaging techniques to measure brain activity before, during, and after acupuncture treatments.

Some experts claim that another alternative therapy, which uses a machine that generates magnetic fields, can alleviate pain. A company called Pico-Tesla, which manufactures a machine called the Resonator, has begun a study to determine whether the machine helps fibromyalgia patients more than medication alone does. The Resonator consists of an elevated platform with a seat for the patient, two circular side panels, and an overhead arch. When the machine is switched on, a generator sends a low-level electromagnetic field over the patient's body. Thus far, the device appears to be safe, though people who are prone to seizures cannot use it because magnetic fields can trigger seizures. Whether it is effective for relieving pain remains to be seen.

A device that sends electrical, rather than magnetic, stimulation into a patient's skin is also being tested. Transcutaneous electrical nerve stimulation (TENS) is known to alleviate pain in some people with cancer, tendonitis, and arthritis, and now researchers at the University of Iowa are studying whether it is effective in people with fibromyalgia. A TENS unit consists of a small battery-powered machine about the size of a calculator.

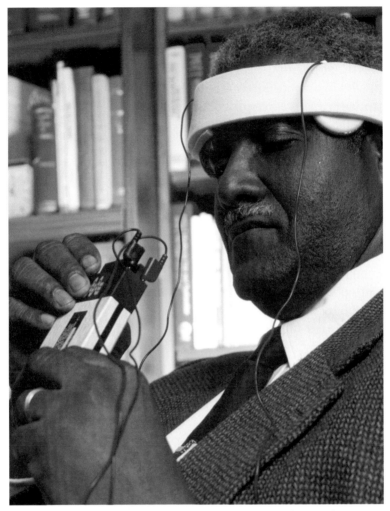

A man uses a transcutaneous electrical nerve stimulator. The nerve stimulator is known to alleviate pain in some people with cancer, tendonitis, and arthritis. Research is in progress to determine whether the device may also be effective in treating FM.

The patient or doctor connects two electrodes from the machine to the patient's skin over a painful area and turns on the device. Some doctors believe the electrical current stimulates nerves and sends signals to the brain that block pain signals. Other experts theorize that the current stimulates the release of natural endorphins.

Another experimental technique that delivers electrical currents is called transcranial direct current stimulation. Here a small battery-powered machine delivers a small electrical current directly into the brain through electrodes placed inside certain brain areas. Because inserting the electrodes is an invasive procedure, and because the current goes directly into the brain, there are serious risks such as brain damage, headache, dizziness, and nausea. However, the current is not painful to patients, and it has been shown to be effective in reducing symptoms in people with Parkinson's disease, anxiety, depression, and stroke. The symptom relief lasts even after the stimulation is discontinued, and doctors can modify the current and electrode placement either to increase or decrease nerve firing, depending on the patient's needs. A group of scientists in Antwerp, Belgium, is currently testing the procedure on fibromyalgia patients who are not helped by other treatments.

One other nondrug therapy being tested is continuous positive airway pressure (CPAP). Doctors prescribe a CPAP device, which consists of a mask hooked up to an air-generating machine, for people who have breathing disorders such as sleep apnea, a condition in which the individual stops breathing repeatedly during sleep. Many people with fibromyalgia continue to experience sleep disruptions even when they take sleeping medications, and some doctors believe this may occur because these people have trouble breathing. As NIAMS explains about a study it is supporting:

> One team has observed that fibromyalgia patients with persistent sleep problems share characteristics with people who have sleep-disordered breathing—a group of disorders, the most common of which is the obstructive sleep apnea, characterized by pauses in breathing during sleep. These researchers are studying whether continuous positive airway pressure (CPAP, a therapy administered by a machine that increases air pressure in the throat to hold it open during sleep) might improve the symptoms of fibromyalgia.[59]

Outlook for the Future

The goals of all the fibromyalgia research and education efforts are to make life easier for the millions of people who have the disease and ultimately to devise a cure. Intertwined with these goals is the hope of patients and advocates that research will prove that fibromyalgia is indeed a real disease that deserves the same attention and respect that other disorders receive. Recent progress in uncovering evidence of biochemical abnormalities in people with fibromyalgia means that the legitimacy controversy may be resolved in the foreseeable future and that new and better treatments that target specific biochemical processes may soon follow. The possibility of a cure also becomes more feasible with each research advance. But while these advances continue to bring medical science closer to achieving these goals, experts acknowledge that there is still much to be done. As the National Fibromyalgia Association states, "Medical researchers have just begun to untangle the truths about this life-altering disease."[60]

Notes

Introduction: A Controversial Disease

1. M. Clement Hall. *The Fibromyalgia Controversy*. New York: Prometheus, 2009, p. 34.
2. George E. Ehrlich. "Pain Is Real, Fibromyalgia Isn't." *Journal of Rheumatology*, August 2003, p. 1,666.
3. Ehrlich. "Pain Is Real, Fibromyalgia Isn't," p. 1,666.
4. Quoted in Hall. *The Fibromyalgia Controversy*, p. 280.
5. Nortin M. Hadler. "Fibromyalgia and the Medicalization of Misery." *Journal of Rheumatology*, August 2003, p. 1,668.
6. Ehrlich. "Pain Is Real, Fibromyalgia Isn't," p. 1,666.
7. Hall. *The Fibromyalgia Controversy*, p. 291.
8. Robert M. Bennett. "Science of Fibromyalgia." National Fibromyalgia Association. www.fmaware.org/site/Page Serverccdf.html?pagename=fibromyalgia_science.

Chapter One: What Is Fibromyalgia?

9. Job 7:3–4, 30:16–17. King James Version.
10. William S. Wilke. *The Cleveland Clinic Guide to Fibromyalgia*. New York: Kaplan, 2010, p. 3.
11. Mayo Clinic. "Fibromyalgia." www.mayoclinic.com/print/fibromyalgia/DS00079/METHOD=print&DSECTION=all.
12. Quoted in Chitale Radha. "Like Chronic Pain, Fibromyalgia Debate Persists." ABC News.com, January 16, 2008. http://abcnews.go.com/Health/PainManagement/story?id=4138715&page=1.
13. Hall. *The Fibromyalgia Controversy*, p. 34.
14. Quoted in Melissa S. Herman. "There Is Something Wrong with Me!" National Fibromyalgia Association, July 5, 2007. www.fmaware.org/site/News21752.html?page=NewsArticle&id=6146.
15. Wilke. *The Cleveland Clinic Guide to Fibromyalgia*, p. 19.

Chapter Two: What Causes Fibromyalgia?

16. American Fibromyalgia Syndrome Association. "What Is Fibromyalgia?" www.afsafund.org/fibromyalgia.html.
17. Quoted in Sharon Ostalecki. *Fibromyalgia: The Complete Guide from Medical Experts and Patients*. Boston: Jones and Bartlett, 2008, p. 188.
18. Wilke. *The Cleveland Clinic Guide to Fibromyalgia*, p. 87.
19. Quoted in Ostalecki. *Fibromyalgia*, p. 9.
20. Harvey Moldofsky. "The Significance, Assessment, and Management of Nonrestorative Sleep in Fibromyalgia Syndrome." CNS Spectrums. www.cnsspectrums.com/aspx/articledetail.aspx?articleid=1497.
21. Quoted in Janis Kelly. "The Significance of Gender." National Fibromyalgia Association. www.fmaware.org/site/News22ec1.html?news_iv_ctrl=1&page=NewsArticle&id=9584.
22. Wilke. *The Cleveland Clinic Guide to Fibromyalgia*, p. viii.
23. Hall. *The Fibromyalgia Controversy*, p. 159.

Chapter Three: How Is Fibromyalgia Treated?

24. National Institute of Arthritis and Musculoskeletal and Skin Diseases. "Fibromyalgia." www.niams.nih.gov/Health_Info/Fibromyalgia/fibromyalgia_ff.asp.
25. Hall. *The Fibromyalgia Controversy*, p. 71.
26. National Institute of Arthritis and Musculoskeletal and Skin Diseases. "Fibromyalgia."
27. Roland Staud. "Pharmaceutical Treatment of Fibromyalgia Syndrome: New Developments." *Drugs*, 2010, p. 1.
28. Wilke. *The Cleveland Clinic Guide to Fibromyalgia*, pp. 100–101.
29. National Institute of Arthritis and Musculoskeletal and Skin Diseases. "Fibromyalgia."
30. Ostalecki. *Fibromyalgia*, p. 234.
31. American Fibromyalgia Syndrome Association. "What Is Fibromyalgia?" www.afsafund.org/fibromyalgia.html.
32. Hall. *The Fibromyalgia Controversy*, p. 123.

33. Wilke. *The Cleveland Clinic Guide to Fibromyalgia*, p. 127.

Chapter Four: Living with Fibromyalgia

34. Bill St. John. "Physical Gains Despite the Pain: A Triathlete with FM Tells His Story." National Fibromyalgia Association, July 5, 2007. www.fmaware.org/site/News 2a54e.html?page=NewsArticle&id=5512.
35. Herman. "There Is Something Wrong with Me!"
36. Irene Leeder. "Your Stories." *Who Cares: Chronic Illness in America*, PBS. www.pbs.org/inthebalance/archives/ whocares/your_stories/irene_leeder.html.
37. Quoted in Ostalecki. *Fibromyalgia*, p. 18.
38. Quoted in Ostalecki. *Fibromyalgia*, p. 180.
39. Quoted in Ostalecki. *Fibromyalgia*, p. 76.
40. Quoted in National Fibromyalgia Association. "Elizabeth Kinzey." November 1, 2007. www.fmaware.org/site/ News22608.html?page=NewsArticle&id=6613.
41. Quoted in National Fibromyalgia Association. "Donna Sellers." www.fmaware.org/site/News2595a.html?page=News Article&id=9103.
42. Quoted in National Fibromyalgia Association. "Brianna Tulin." February 29, 2009. www.fmaware.org/site/ News2f28b.html?page=NewsArticle&id=8581.
43. John Fry. "How to Be a Better Friend, Spouse, or Relative to Someone with FM." National Fibromyalgia Association, June 21, 2007. www.fmaware.org/site/News25eaf .html?page=NewsArticle&id=6040.
44. Kristine Creamer-Pardieu. "A Better Life Worth Living." National Fibromyalgia Association, July 5, 2007. www .fmaware.org/site/News25b3e.html?page=NewsArticle &id=6143.
45. Melissa Olivadoti. "Education Helps Her Increase Awareness." National Fibromyalgia Association, July 5, 2007. www.fmaware.org/site/News25c1c.html?page=News Article&id=6093.
46. Quoted in National Fibromyalgia Association. "Nicole Sloan." www.fmaware.org/site/News2cdf8.html?page= NewsArticle&id=7265.

47. National Fibromyalgia Association. "Support Group Information." www.fmaware.org/site/PageServer124c. html?pagename=community_supportGroupInformation.
48. Jennifer Herman. "In This Together." National Fibromyalgia Association, June 11, 2007. www.fmaware.org/site/News2ed12.html?page=NewsArticle&id=6038.
49. Quoted in National Fibromyalgia Association. "'Team Fibro Fighter' Honored at National Fibromyalgia Awareness Day." www.fmaware.org/site/News28d0b.html?news_iv_ctrl=-1&page=NewsArticle&id=9608.
50. Quoted in National Fibromyalgia Association. "'Team Fibro Fighter' Honored at National Fibromyalgia Awareness Day."
51. Quoted in National Fibromyalgia Association. "Brianna Tulin."

Chapter Five: The Future

52. Quoted in National Fibromyalgia Association. "Men with FM." www.fmaware.org/site/News22742.html?news_iv_ctrl=1&page=NewsArticle&id=9582.
53. National Fibromyalgia Association. "Economic Burden." National Fibromyalgia Association. www.fmaware.org/site/PageServeraa5e.html?pagename=fibromyalgia_economicBurden.
54. National Fibromyalgia Association. "Prognosis." www.fmaware.org/site/PageServer54c5. html?pagename=fibromyalgia_prognosis.
55. Quoted in American Fibromyalgia Syndrome Association. "Electrocardiogram-Based Sleep Spectrogram." www.afsafund.org/update1109.html.
56. Quoted in American Fibromyalgia Syndrome Association. "Role of Myofascial Trigger Points in FMS—Part 2." www.afsafund.org/update1109.html.
57. American Fibromyalgia Syndrome Association. "Genetic Influences on Pain Modulation Systems in Fibromyalgia." www.afsafund.org/update1109.html.
58. University of Utah. "Nutrition and Coping Education for Symptoms and Weight Management for Fibromyalgia." Clinical Trials.gov. http://clinicaltrials.gov/ct2/show/NC

T00925431?recr=Open&cond=%22Fibromyalgia%22&r
ank=34.

59. National Institute of Arthritis and Musculoskeletal and
    Skin Diseases. "Fibromyalgia." www.niams.nih.gov/
    Health_Info/Fibromyalgia/default.asp.

60. National Fibromyalgia Association. "Causes." www.fm
    aware.org/site/PageServer06af.html?pagename=fibro
    myalgia_causes.

Glossary

allodynia: A condition in which sensations that are not normally unpleasant feel painful.

autonomic nervous system: The part of the nervous system not under voluntary control.

axon: A long extension on a nerve cell that transmits signals to other nerve cells.

biomarker: A chemical or physical indicator that can be used to diagnose or assess changes in a disease.

central nervous system: The brain and spinal cord.

cerebrospinal fluid: The liquid that surrounds the brain and spinal cord.

chromosome: A structure in the center of each cell where genes reside.

dendrite: A short extension on a nerve cell that receives signals from other nerve cells.

depression: Prolonged feelings of hopelessness, helplessness, sadness, and disinterest.

dolorimeter: An instrument that measures pain levels at various points throughout the body.

fibromyalgia: A chronic disease characterized by widespread pain, fatigue, and overly sensitive nerves.

gene: The part of a DNA molecule that transmits hereditary information from parents to their offspring.

myofascial trigger points: Firm, painful knots in the muscles from which pain radiates to other areas.

neuron: A nerve cell.

neurotransmitter: A chemical messenger in the nervous system.

nociceptor: A specialized nerve ending that senses and transmits pain signals.

parasympathetic nervous system: The part of the autonomic nervous system that calms the body's reaction to stress.

peripheral nervous system: Nerves outside the brain and spinal cord.

rheumatologist: A doctor who specializes in treating painful diseases affecting the muscles and skeleton.

sensitization: Enhanced feelings of pain and overstimulation of nerves.

sympathetic nervous system: The part of the autonomic nervous system that mobilizes the body to fight or flee from stress.

tender points: Places throughout the body a doctor presses on to assess pain in diagnosing fibromyalgia.

voluntary nervous system: The part of the nervous system under conscious control.

Organizations to Contact

American Fibromyalgia Syndrome Association (AFSA)

7371 E. Tanque Verde Rd.
Tucson, AZ 85715
(520) 733-1570
www.afsafund.org

The AFSA is the leading nonprofit organization dedicated solely to funding fibromyalgia research. It also provides general information to patients and the public.

Centers for Disease Control and Prevention (CDC)

Arthritis Program
Mailstop K-51
4770 Buford Hwy. NE
Atlanta, GA 30341-3724
(770) 488-5464
www.cdc.gov/arthritis/basics/fibromyalgia.htm

The CDC is a public health agency that provides statistics and comprehensive information on all aspects of fibromyalgia and other diseases.

National Fibromyalgia Association (NFA)

2121 South Towne Center Pl., Ste. 300
Anaheim, CA 92806
(714) 921-0150
www.fmaware.org

The NFA is the largest nonprofit organization dedicated to increasing public awareness of fibromyalgia and providing information, support, and advocacy for patients and their families.

National Institute of Arthritis and Musculoskeletal and Skin Diseases (NIAMS)

Information Clearinghouse
National Institutes of Health
1 AMS Cir.
Bethesda, MD 20892-3675
(301) 495-4484; toll-free: 877-226-4267
www.niams.nih.gov

The NIAMS is the primary government agency that sponsors and promotes research on fibromyalgia. It also furnishes information on all aspects of the disease.

For More Information

Books

Sylvia Engdahl. *Fibromyalgia*. Farmington Hills, MI: Green-
haven, 2010. Written for teens; discusses controversies sur-
rounding fibromyalgia and general information about the
disease.

Bryan C. Hains. *Pain*. New York: Chelsea House, 2007. Written
for teens; discusses the biological mechanisms that underlie
pain, disorders that affect pain, and treatments.

Internet Sources

Radha Chitale. "Like Chronic Pain, Fibromyalgia Debate Persists." ABC News.com, January 16, 2008. http://abcnews
.go.com/Health/PainManagement/story?id=4138715&page=1
. National Fibromyalgia Association. "Brianna Tulin." February 29, 2009. www.fmaware.org/site/News2f28b.html?page=
NewsArticle&id=8581.

National Fibromyalgia Association. "Elizabeth Kinzey." November 1, 2007. www.fmaware.org/site/News22608.html?
page=NewsArticle&id=6613.

WebMD. "Fibromyalgia in Children and Teens." www.webmd
.com/fibromyalgia/guide/fibromyalgia-in-children-and-
teens.

Websites

**"Bones, Muscles, and Joints: The Musculoskeletal Sys-
tem," TeensHealth** (http://kidshealth.org/teen/your_body/
body_basics/bones_muscles_joints.html#cat20120). Teen
website about bones, muscles, and joints, which have rel-
evance to fibromyalgia.

"Brain and Nervous System," **TeensHealth** (http://kid shealth.org/teens/diseases_conditions/body_basics/brain_nervous_system.html#cat20155). Teen website about the nervous system, which weighs heavily in fibromyalgia.

"Fibromyalgia," **National Institute of Arthritis and Musculoskeletal and Skin Diseases** (www.niams.nih.gov/Health_Info/Fibromyalgia/fibromyalgia_ff.asp). Easily understood overview of fibromyalgia.

"Stress," **TeensHealth** (http://kidshealth.org/teen/your_mind/emotions/stress.html). Teen website about stress, which plays a role in fibromyalgia.

Index

Picture Credits

Cover: Jim Dowdalls/Photo Researchers, Inc.
© 2010StockVS/Alamy, 20
AJPhoto/Photo Researchers, Inc., 39
Alfred Pasieka/Photo Researchers, Inc., 8
© allOver photography/Alamy, 73
AP Images/Al Goldis, 65
AP Images/PRNewsFoto/Eli Lilly and Company, 91
BSIP/Photo Researchers, Inc., 22, 29, 31
© Chad Ehlers/Alamy, 57
© David Hoffman Photo Library/Alamy, 89
© David R. Gee/Alamy, 49
Gale, Cengage Learning, 18, 41
Hank Morgan/Photo Researchers, Inc., 93
Jim Varney/Photo Researchers, Inc., 45
John T. Fowler/Alamy, 60
Life in View/Photo Researchers, Inc., 86
© mediacolor's/Alamy, 58
Nancy Kedersha/Photo Researchers, Inc., 83
© Nucleus Medical Art, Inc./Alamy, 16
© Peter Titmuss/Alamy, 69
Philippe Garo/Photo Researchers, Inc., 42
© Photofusion Picture Library/Alamy, 54
© Picture Partners/Alamy, 52
© PoodlesRock/Corbis, 12
© Ralph Henning/Alamy, 63
Richard T. Nowitz/Photo Researchers, Inc., 76
Robin Conn/The Huntsville Times/Landov, 79
Scott Carmazine/Photo Researchers, Inc., 36
SSPL/Getty Images, 15
© Visuals Unlimited/Corbis, 33

About the Author

Melissa Abramovitz has been writing books, magazine articles, short stories, and poems for children, teens, and adults for twenty-five years. Many of her works are on health topics.

She grew up in San Diego, California, and developed an interest in medical topics as a teenager. At one time she thought she wanted to become a doctor but later switched her major and earned a degree in psychology from the University of California at San Diego in 1976. She began writing professionally in 1986 to allow her to be an at-home mom when her two children were small.